Dedication

To all those people, living and dead, who have helped me arrive at this point in my life.

O My Soul

O My Soul

The Inside Story

Tom Peters [signature]

by
Tom Peters

Foreword by Bishop William M. Cosgrove

betterpubpress
606 Middle Ave., Elyria, Ohio 44035
216-323-2431

PERMISSIONS

The following publishers have generously given permission to use extended quotations from copyrighted works: Reprinted by permission of the publishers and the trustees of Amherst College from the *The Poems of Emily Dickinson*, Thomas H. Johnson, ed., Cambridge, Mass.: The Belknap Press of Harvard University Press, Copyright 1951, 1955, 1979, 1983, by the Presidential Fellows of Harvard College. Excerpts from the English translation of *The Liturgy of the Hours* © 1974, International Committee on English in the Liturgy, Inc. all rights reserved. Permission, Sheed and Ward, Illustrations from Ade Bethune's *Eye Contact With God. Grail Psalms*, Ladies of the Grail (English), used by permission of G.I.A. Publications, Inc. Chicago, Ill. exclusive agent, all rights reserved. Excerpts from THE JERUSALEM BIBLE, copyright © 1966 by Darton, Longman & Todd, Ltd., and Doubleday, a division of Bantam Doubleday Dell Publishing Group, Inc. Reprinted by permission. *Proud Donkey of Schaerbeek* by Judith Stoughton, North Star Press of St. Cloud, illustrations from collection of Ade Bethune.

Copyright © 1991 by Tom Peters

ISBN 1-879516-00-4

Library of Congress Catalog Card Number: 90-085896

606 Middle Ave., Elyria, Ohio 44035
216-323-2431

Table of Contents

Foreword   ix
Preface   xi
Acknowledgments   xiii
Introduction   xv

Part I   Trials and Tribulations

1. Guilty and Not Guilty   3
2. The Trial   7
3. The Sentencing and the Appeal   11

Part II   The Pre-Trial Years

4. The Catholics in My Family   15
5. The Protestant Side of my Family:
   Peters and Huntley   24
6. Marriage, Birth, and Early Schooling   30
7. High School, Forest View Farm, and Oberlin   39
8. Dayton, A Cemetery, Death   45
9. The "Little Sem" and the Novitiate   49
10. St. Charles Seminary, Summers in Appalachia,
    Father Connors   56
11. St. Mary's Seminary, Notre Dame University,
    and Chicago   62
12. Seminary Days End, Farming, Social Work   69
13. Boston College, Harvard, Cape Cod   74
14. Back in Lorain, Street Clubs   79
15. Gangs and Cursillos   84
16. Mexico, Guadalupe   90
17. Marriage, a Honeymoon to Chicago, Mexico Again   94
18. Betterway Grows, and Grows, and Grows.   100

19. The Cleveland Foundation: The Cleveland Scene	106
20. Europe	110
21. Canada	116
22. Back to Betterway: The Deli, the Farm, the Trolley, New Programs	121
23. Cape Cod, Key West, Gethsemani, Prisons	126
24. Cemeteries and Death	134
25. Communion with the Dead	140
26. Books	146
27. In the Public Eye	151
28. Summing It Up	154

Part III Into The Fiery Furnace

29. August 8, 1988	159
30. The Struggle Begins	165
31. Going Public; The First Spiritual Crisis	170
32. Spiritual Developments: Mary	176
33. The Eucharist, the Poor Clares, and Eternity	181
34. The Bible	186
35. "Get Out of the Way"	190
36. Indicted; Leaving	195
37. Writing, Books, Courts, and Funerals	201
38. Oberlin College: Chromosomes and Monasteries	206
39. Humiliation and Forgiveness	212
40. Icons and Maronites	218
41. More Books: *The Last Things*; The *Song of Songs*	223
42. Return to Betterway	228
43. Visiting the Dead and the Not So Dead	233
44. The Wheels of Justice	240
45. Endings and Beginnings	245

Epilogue	250

Foreword

By Bishop William M. Cosgrove,
Retired Bishop of Belleville, Illinois

Bishop William M. Cosgrove

The unbelievable indictment of Tom Peters led to my frequent talking with Tom. I eventually encouraged him to write down some of the events of his 60 years of living. I have known Tom for almost 30 years but we have become close friends only during this time.

Tom had led an extremely interesting life and the more I visited with him, the more value I saw in making his life experiences available to other people. I have never met a person who has come into contact with so many interesting and influential people: little people, professional people, troubled people, wealthy people, phony people, dishonest people, inspiring people, greedy people, saintly people.

Not only did Tom meet this great variety of folks, but he has the unusual ability to listen, to learn, to draw out, and when necessary to respond to the needs of the fragile people the good Lord seemed to send his way or Tom sought out.

In spite of the pain which Tom, his wife, Mary, his family and friends have experienced during this past year, I am convinced that the pain, like the pain of childbirth, will help give life to new responses to different fragile people than he has served in the past. The pain seems to have had the opposite effect than we would ordinarily expect. It has not been the occasion for depression, withdrawal from society, or hatred for his accusers. Instead, it has enabled him to associate it with the sufferings of Christ and has been the opportunity for great growth in the spiritual life. His dependence upon prayer and the Sacraments of his Catholic faith has enabled him to be very peaceful in a situation which usually brings about great stress.

He has been an inspiration to me and I thank God that I came to Elyria at this time in my life, if for no other reason than to be close to Tom during these times.

I pray that justice will prevail in the months to come. Tom's ministry to troubled youth is no longer a unique service. Others have imitated the pioneer efforts which created Betterway. Given the opportunity, Tom looked for new challenges to respond to the needs of fragile people. He searched out ways to respond to the homeless, the poor families, and those with AIDS.

A few months before Tom was indicted, and there was no hint that he might be a target of some police, I appeared before the Elyria, Ohio City Council without Tom's previous knowledge or the advice of anyone else. When the decision was made by council to limit the expansion of the Betterway Program, my statement basically said that we need more people like Tom Peters.

I still make this statement with even greater emphasis. Now that the special ministry to youth provided by Betterway has been transferred to others, the way is open to even more important ministries, perhaps helping many more people by publishing books like this one.

I do not know what the future holds for Tom, but I believe he will respond in ways that will be similar to the past, and meaningful to others.

Preface

This is the story of a life lived mostly in Elyria, Ohio. Elyria is a small city by world comparison, about 60,000 people. Elyria is not even 200 years old.

This is a small story by world comparison. Other lives are more dramatic, have a greater impact on humanity. But for me it is everything. It is all that I am.

This is a story of part of my life, an inner part, the spiritual part.

We are on a physical and spiritual journey through life. We are body and spirit joined to form one person. Sometimes circumstances bring out the spiritual side more clearly. This is what happened in my life.

I was confronted with a crisis in which I had to use all the spiritual resources of my life to survive. I say spiritual resources, still realizing the spirit and body are together and that it was the whole me that worked in this survival. The spirit part of Tom Peters is not separate from the body of Tom Peters. My body would not be mine without my spirit.

This book is divided into three parts: the trial, the preparation, and the fiery furnace.

The idea to write a book came from Bill Cosgrove, the retired Roman Catholic Bishop of Belleville, Illinois, who was living in Elyria, Ohio. During the year-and-a-half of crisis, he became my helper and friend. In the Spring of 1989 he said I should write down what was happening to me.

This was written mostly over a two month time in the early summer of 1989, a few chapters every day, from notes I began keeping in January of that year.

All life is a drama; in a way, a trial. I think all life is also like a pursuit between our Creator and ourselves. We are drawn to our Creator and our Creator is drawn to us. That is the central mystery in our life, the heart of it all for each one of us. We are being smelted, as ore in a furnace.

The Lord is the hound of heaven, chasing us down until we are His. And we like to be chased, we tease and chase back. We are two lovers, always in pursuit of one another. Tried and true at the end.

This book is the story of some of that chase for me. I hope it helps the reader in the trial of life, the crisis, the pursuit. I hope it helps some people, who may be afraid, to sense the joy at the end of the chase.

"Be not afraid, I am with you always. Come, follow me."

The spiritual inspiration for my life is my Catholic religion. It is the faith of my birth. Others are equally inspired by their religion, Judaism, Hinduism, Buddhism, Islam, and the various Protestant Christian faiths. The center of all these is the Creator, and the ways we relate to the Creator and to the people in our lives who are visible reflections of the Creator.

Because I am Catholic I write from that perspective. I also appreciate and love many parts of other religions. I hope the readers of this book, who belong to other religions, or no religion at all, can love and enjoy my beliefs through me. I hope this will strengthen their own beliefs to help them cope with their life struggles.

I AM THE
RESURRECTION
AND THE LIFE

Acknowledgments

I thank Bishop William Cosgrove, who gave me the idea to do this book and helped in the struggle described here.

My wife Mary and daughter Pam who read it, gave ideas, and put it on the computer disk.

Mike Gonsziorowski, a Betterway board member, who read it and helped with ideas. And his wife, Joy.

Bill Scrivo, who I knew when he was managing editor at the Lorain Journal, edited this material. He is presently Public Relations Director for the Better Business Bureau in Cleveland.

The illustrations are by Ade Bethune, a longtime favorite of mine.

Finally, I acknowledge the help of Professional Book Compositors who took this from disc to the finished book.

Introduction

I am a social worker who likes to write, talk, walk, and pray. I also like to plan and start new ideas and have been doing all of these things all of my adult life. I was born March 29, 1929, fifty-nine years ago, as I write this.

My spiritual life began to develop in my late teens when I became seriously ill, and then progressed through six years of seminary training. I left that world two years before becoming a priest and entered into social work, which became my life theme. There were other sicknesses, and ups-and-downs in my spiritual life.

By the age of 59 my world seemed to be going along in a routine way until August, 1988. I was founder and director of Betterway, a social service agency operating six group homes for teenage boys and girls, a string of foster homes, a restaurant, a gift shop, a Victorian trolley for local tours, and a 150 acre rural retreat property. They were all in Northern Ohio, west of Cleveland, in my home town of Elyria. The rural place is 15 miles south, in Wellington. I named the agency Betterway shortly after it started, 24 years earlier.

I had been writing a Sunday newspaper column, "Like It Is," in my home-town newspaper for 20 years. Area papers did numerous features on our work over the years and television stations did three documentaries about us. I was editor of a newspaper, called Betterway, going out to 20,000 people.

We were the first in the world to have group homes in the community for boys and girls in trouble. Up to 1965 such youth were placed in foster homes or large public and private institutions. The group home movement grew from our first homes and has spread everywhere. Group homes are part of most cities today.

We were mostly well accepted, although there were a few

lawsuits when we bought the rural property and occasional letters to the editor over some incident around a group home.

We employed 65 people, had a budget of $2 million a year with no federal funds. Private grants were used to start new programs. We raised our own operating expenses through our fees and businesses.

All did not remain well. In 1986 we bought two new group homes a few blocks from our four other ones, but on a new street. This brought petitions and some angry meetings at city council. Then a staff person was attacked in one of our girls' group homes at night. The suspect was an 18 year-old black youth from one of our other homes. He had been put out of Boys Town in Omaha as a senior when he got involved with a girl resident. He was conceited, and an easy-to-dislike suspect.

The woman was white, very popular in town, the founder and leader of a well-known drill team. Scientific tests proved that this boy could not have been involved and he was eventually freed. This made some people very angry, including some police.

In 1988 Betterway purchased a replica of a Victorian trolley to use for tours and rent for public or private events, such as parades. This was bought from money we saved but it seemed to some to indicate we had secret sources of funds.

Betterway staff were asked questions and heard comments about all these things around town.

During this same time a committee of city council started legislative procedures to limit the growth of group homes. The committee passed a law that future homes had to be a certain distance apart, meaning no more could be started in our part of the city in the large older homes.

At the same time the police department initiated an investigation of me. This went on for months and included periodic "leaks" to the newspapers about forthcoming sex charges, illustrated by photographs.

The investigation began in August, 1988, but was not revealed to the media until November. The two local newspapers, the Cleveland paper, and a half-dozen television stations and many other papers and radio stations across Ohio and in some other states began to carry stories about my connection to nude photos, implying there were hundreds. They also indicated that boys were telling horror tales to the detective.

Referrals of boys and girls to our homes were halted because of all the publicity. Speeches I had scheduled were cancelled.

People looked at me in a new way.

In late December of 1988 I was indicted for 24 misdemeanor counts of touching boys in "erogenous zones" and taking nude photos, one felony count. I took a leave from Betterway, hoping this would keep the placing agencies from removing the boys and girls from our homes. None were removed, but no new ones came, so gradually the homes were emptied and four were closed as we moved into 1989.

I was home and off work from Dec. 30, 1988 until April 20, 1989. I returned to work on the feast of Passover, but my ordeal was not past. From January until July 3, 1989, there were a series of pretrials and hearings on my case.

During this entire time I had to return to my spiritual roots and habits to survive. I had to build on the past. Over the year I felt one crisis after another as the media featured my story frequently, emphasizing the sexual implications, using legal sexual terms to describe my crimes, often on the front page with my photo.

* * * * * * * * *

Our spiritual roots are part of our entire history, even the history of our parents, our birth, our early life. We do not suddenly have a spiritual side or suddenly discover God and prayer and beliefs about morals and an existence after death. These concepts grow as we grow.

I think life is like a mosaic, a painting, a tapestry. We see it piece by piece, section by section, like an artist. It is not until it is finished and we step back that all the little threads or the spots of paint and color come together to make the scene of our own life.

It seems to me that the first 59 years of my life prepared me to survive the really difficult days in 1988 and 1989 and beyond. Even the lives of my parents before I was born were part of the influence on me. When life is over for me I know I will see that even the events of this intense experience of a public investigation and public trial will have prepared me for what is yet to come. They will also be part of the finished picture.

I won't understand how the present events created that final scene until it is all finished, but in this book I want to share with readers my inner life, my soul's life, to the time of 1990.

Although I was a Roman Catholic from birth, and in tradition, on my mother's side of the family, as I grew into adulthood I found that I had a kind of "conversion" to adult Roman Catholic ways, examining intellectually and in prayer my religion, to see if it would be part of my adult life and not just accepted like a child. It then became the religion of my choice, my belief, my love. Here is my story.

Part I

Trials and Tribulations

Peters changes mind, asks trial

Judge to rule Monday on bid to quash sex case guilty plea

Peters will go on trial in Elyria sex case

Peters accuser: 'That's me' in the nude photo

Peters cleared of sex felony

Cop has 'no hard feelings'

Betterway founder will be sentenced on misdemeanors

Peters guilty on 16 charges

Jury finds him innocent on felony count

Betterway founder convicted on sex counts

Peters is sentenced to 2½ years in jail

Quirk in state law reduces time to 18 months

Prosecutors: Put Peters in state prison

Peters slapped with 18 months in jail

Chapter 1

Guilty and Not Guilty

Guilty!
Guilty!
Guilty!
Guilty!
Guilty!
Guilty!
Guilty!
Guilty!
Guilty!
Guilty!
Guilty!
Guilty!
Guilty!
Guilty!
Not Guilty!
Guilty!
Guilty!

Before each declaration the judge read the charge against me, then pronounced the decision of the jury.

It was a little after 8:30 on a cold, wet night on the first of December, 1989. It was hard for me to believe this event was happening. I sat directly behind my attorney, occasionally looking at the back of his head to see if there was any reaction. Other times I looked up at the judge, a high school acquaintance of mine. A man I saw frequently going to his office near Betterway's Deli restaurant, or driving home as Mary and I took our evening walk.

Now he sat in his black robes intoning "guilty" so many times.

It seems like I should have turned around to look at my family, to tell them not to feel bad, or to look at the detective and the prosecutor seated a few feet to my right at the same table. But I did not look anywhere except at the back of my attorney's unflinching head in front of me and up at the judge.

Then it was over. The members of the jury were uneasy and not looking up. They seemed to avoid contact with me and left quickly. Only the foreman had a smile on his face. For a full week, hours every day, they sat and stared at me, at my attorney, and at the others in the small courtrooms. They became an intimate part of my life and suddenly they disappeared. I wanted to talk with them, to see how they decided, to see them as fellow human beings. Citizens of my county, a jury of my peers.

I stood up after all the "guilties" and shook the hand of my attorney. The "not guilty" had been on the one felony charge which would have sent me to prison. The "guilties" were on 16 misdemeanor charges. Before dismissing everyone, the judge granted me freedom on bond until the sentencing in two weeks. That would be Dec. 15.

I turned around and walked over to my family and a few friends and a dozen reporters. Now I said "Don't feel too bad," to my family and to anyone who cared, and to myself too.

The dozen or so reporters and television people gathered around my attorney and I, and my wife. Would we appeal? Probably. How did I feel? No comment. Was I surprised? No comment. What else did I have to say? Nothing.

I then fell into small talk with my family and we decided to go over to the home of our son and visit. It was like the time after the funeral of a relative. Before leaving the courthouse my wife and I met with the attorney in the small room where the jury had deliberated for four hours. The long table was littered with cigarette butts and styrofoam coffee cups, messy looking, confining. The room was dirty.

The three of us talked over the mechanics of an appeal but we were all too exhausted to think much. After we got the bare outlines we went out of the dark building into the cold, and to our cars.

* * * * * * * * *

The trial had ended with the closing arguments about 4 p.m. that Friday. My family and I stayed around for an hour or so to see if the jury might reach a quick verdict. My attorney and his wife, who had been present for the whole trial, went to get a bite at a local watering hole for attorneys, less than a block away.

There was no quick verdict, so we went home with our two sons and daughter. The time went slowly. It was another waiting time, like many times in the year-and-a-half since the investigation began. Pre-trials, hearings, arraignment, indictment. Words that did not mean much to me before but now had real life definition.

The wait that night at our house was like a time warp. It did not seem real.

Mary, my wife of 25 years was there. Our sons Tom and Don, and his twin, Pam. Tom ran the Deli restaurant for Betterway and had been at most of the trial while his wife Karen was home with their little girl. Don, who is single, came up from Athens, Ohio, where he lays tile and was at the entire trial. Pam came most of the time. She lives in Elyria and cares for her three children, including a new one. Her husband, Jack, watched the kids.

* * * * * * * * *

At Tom and Karen's house that night we talked about the week-long trial, trying to decide how the jury reached its verdicts, rehashing what seemed important in the five days of the trial; what might have been done differently.

After a few hours we guessed we had it talked out as much as possible that close to the event. We would learn more later, but for now we were exhausted. We comforted one another as much as we could. Mary and I went home and talked a little more and fell into bed for a little reading and then sleep. We were too tired to think about it anymore.

The next morning, a Saturday, the local papers came out with headlines, one saying I was found guilty,; the other that I was innocent of the felony. Two contrasting headlines, with big color photos catching me with my head tilted down. Most of the time my head was looking up, but catching this moment made me look more guilty.

The much larger Cleveland paper had me guilty, but not in headlines. Events in Lorain County rarely merit headlines in the Cleveland Plain Dealer. With a circulation in Ohio of almost a million readers, the Cleveland papers announced the guilty finding to a lot more people.

But nothing mattered too much now. I didn't feel too bad. It was over. At least this part.

Chapter 2

The Trial

In August of 1988 a new Elyria detective began to investigate me.

A 15 year old boy who had been at Betterway a few months left, and then had to return. He told other boys and staff he was going to say I had molested him so he would be put out of our group home and get a foster home. He did not want to come back to a group home.

He told his caseworker just that. The caseworker reported it to the county welfare officials, who reported it to the police, who assigned it to the new detective, who was the stepnephew of the councilman who passed the legislation against group homes. He was raised by the councilman's brother.

The boy was removed to another placement, much to the surprise of many other youth in the six Betterway group homes. It was kind of simple.

Others had said they wanted to go here or there for months longer than this boy and they were not removed like that. To kids in group homes and child care institutions, the grass often seems greener somewhere else. Actually, most of them would like to be home and hate being anywhere else. They tend to blame where they are for not being home, and in a sense this is true. If there was nowhere to go, they would be left at home.

A few weeks later a second Betterway boy was on his way to the detention home from the same group home after being a suspect in stealing one or more cars, getting drunk numerous times, threatening staff, and bragging to the other boys on his escapades.

He told some court staff the reason he did all this was "because Tom Peters had molested him." The court people believed this, even though the boy had a history of emotional and criminal behavior and had been in Ohio's institution for the most mentally disturbed delinquent youth.

The third and final element entering in the investigation was the existence of five photos showing the sex areas of males. The males could not be identified and no other people were in the photos. A Betterway boy told the detective that the photos existed in another boy's folder in his group home, and that they came from a former foster home of that boy, stolen to show the kind of home it was so the boy would not have to return there. They had been kept in the boy's file several years at the request of his caseworker and everyone knew about them.

The detective obtained these photos through a boy in the group home.

In early November, about 10 police conducted a raid on that group home and my office to find more photos. None were found, but the raid was "leaked" to the press, I was declared the subject of the investigation and it was stated I took the sex photos.

The detective then interviewed many more boys, asking them to help get me put away, and to tell him if I had ever touched them, hugged them, kissed them.

Some boys said I had hugged and kissed them and evidence was gathered. Boys were interviewed for months, some having been at Betterway going back four years but now long gone. Former staff gave the names and locations of boys, including some in prisons. An 18 year-old in prison, after being interviewed twice by the detective, said he recognized one of the sex photos as one that I took of him after getting him "high" in my office. This person had been in 40 institutions since the age of 9. He had been at Betterway for 23 days in 1985. But he played an important part in the investigation and the charges.

In late December of 1988 I was indicted for 12 misdemeanor counts of sexually touching boys, twelve misdemeanor counts of asking to touch them (sexual imposition and sexual importuning) and one felony count of taking a sexual photo of a boy. I was arrested and began a long series of steps in January of 1989 that led to a criminal trial starting on November 27, 1989, the Monday after Thanksgiving. There were 60 articles and some front page photos of me in each of the local newspapers by then, and some in other papers.

The jury was seated on that first trial day. Almost everyone on the jury had heard of the investigation and charges but stated they did not have prejudiced opinions.

The second day began with boys who testified that I touched them on the thigh.

Two former staff testified that I showed favoritism, that I bought things for boys and gave out candy. One man testified that I told him I was guilty and expected to go to prison. He portrayed himself as a family friend.

After the state's witnesses finished, my wife testified on my behalf, then I took the stand. The councilman was called to the witness stand as my attorney tried to show a connection between people who seemed to be against Betterway's group homes and the investigation and charges against me.

On the fifth day of the trial I was cross examined by the prosecutor, closing arguments were given by both sides and the case went to the jury for their decision.

Chapter 3

The Sentencing and The Appeal

The two weeks from the end of the trial to the sentencing date passed like the other waiting times. There is nothing one can do to hasten the moment to come. It was the same waiting for the investigation to end, waiting for the indictment, waiting for the arraignment, waiting for each hearing, each pretrial. For me it was a great teacher of patience and trust in God, who already knows the outcome of each event.

I was now officially pronounced "guilty." The detective and others had interviews in the paper saying how they had just done their job, wondering if other youth were out there needing "to talk" like the seven in the trial. Someone "leaked" to one paper that the jury felt I did take "sex photos" but not the exact photos seen by the jury in the trial.

I spent the time talking with various people and doing the work of running Betterway, knowing I might not be free in the community after Dec. 15th.

That day a major snowstorm developed in northern Ohio and by the sentencing time of 2:30 in the afternoon it was a blizzard. This prevented the TV people from driving out from Cleveland and kept the reporters and photographers down to a half dozen.

The sentencing was in the courtroom of the judge who

heard the case. The trial had moved in and out of two other courtrooms because of prior commitments in each room.

My family gathered again, along with my attorney, the detective, the prosecutor, and a few spectators. The mood in the room was quiet, and people were probably distracted by the heavily falling snow, wondering how much we would get, what would close, would there be school? All this goes with a winter storm.

The papers had carried articles that I might be sentenced to a state prison for the misdemeanors. The prosecutor had requested this, saying I did violence to the boys. The proceedings got underway. My attorney pleaded for my probation, the prosecutor argued for prison. The judge ruled that I would not go to a state prison, made a few other comments and then my attorney told me to stand, with him, for the actual sentencing. The various charges were read off with various sentences for each, totaling 2 1/2 years in the local jail, and $4,000 in fines. Since a person can only stay in a local jail for 18 months in Ohio, it amounted to 18 months in jail. I turned red, and it was over.

In closing, the judge said I would report to the jail after the holidays, Jan. 2. Another wait. My attorney said he would be entering an appeal, the judge continued my bond, and I turned again to my family to talk. It seemed like an empty time. No one rejoiced, no one wept, but everyone was serious looking. We drove home in the storm.

Now that I was sentenced, some people expected me to leave the community for prison and they tried to figure out ways to say goodbye or offer their sympathy. Surprisingly there were no crank calls at work or at home, saying I got what I deserved. And no hate mail. There had been some of this during the prior year and a half, but not now.

In fact, I was becoming better known and liked by some. A few days before the sentencing I went to Sacred Heart Chapel in Lorain to celebrate the feast of Our Lady of Guadalupe, a Mexican feast, my favorite.

The people received me warmly, with hugs and affection and wishes of support. After the liturgy a young man, about 20, with a heavy Puerto Rican New York accent came up to me and pointed, saying he had seen me on television. He said this over and over, finally declaring he knew I had a quiz program. What one was it? "What's you quiz program, man?" After asking a string of times, I told him he had seen me on TV during my trial. He got a wide-eyed knowing look and said yes, that was it, then in a direct way said, "Did you do it?" I said no and he shook my hand and rejoiced with a laugh and a thumbs up sign, saying "Alright."

During the week of the trial I could scarcely pray or think of anything else, I was so caught up in the drama of the event, seeing old friends, seeing boys I had worked with over the years now testifying against me, watching the jury, the reporters, talking with my family, meeting at night with my attorney. It was totally absorbing.

In the weeks before sentencing, and the holidays before I was to report to jail, I returned to the pattern of life I had developed during the almost 16 months of the investigation before the trial. My life was calm, my days ordered, my spirits good.

On January 2, I did not report to jail at 8 a.m. My attorney had filed an appeal, the judge continued the bond. I went to work that day at Betterway after attending morning Mass at St. Jude's church in Elyria.

Part II

Prep-Time

Chapter 4

The Catholics in My Family

This is the story of my mother's family, as I heard and read about it. This heritage is part of my spiritual life.

On my mother's father's side was my Irish grandfather, Jim Moroney, whose parents came from County Limerick in Ireland. That's up the Shannon River on the Western side of Ireland, which faces the U.S.A. Grandfather Jim married Rosalee Wimmers, my grandmother. The Wimmers were German, so my grandparents were Irish and German on my mother's side. They died before I was born.

From family stories I learned that Grandfather Jim was a handsome Irishman and a heavy drinker. He was a street car conductor on the line that went from Elyria to Cleveland. At one time in his life he and some friends bought a bar in Elyria and drank up all the contents. The venture ended shortly after. Photos of Jim show him with a large handlebar mustache.

When he was drinking Jim would sometimes get very angry and become violently physical with his family. Rosalee suffered from this. She was a tiny woman. One of my mother's treasures at home is a pair of white shoes worn by Grandmother Rosalee on her wedding day. They seem like doll shoes. Jim had a brother named Dennis, who had a son by the same name who presently owns the fish market at the West Side Market, a Cleveland, Ohio, landmark. The fish-market-Moroney has a son, Tom Moroney, who is now an attorney in

Oberlin, Ohio, with numerous little Irish Moroneys in his family. I shop at the fish market almost weekly.

The father of Jim and Dennis had a brother who settled in the Kipton, Ohio, rural area near Elyria with 50 other Irish immigrant families. They were called "Shanty Irish." Many worked on laying the first tracks of the New York Central Railroad. These families are buried in the cemetery in nearby Wakeman, Ohio, and had names like O'Connell, O'Grady, Murray, Maroney, and Moroney, and first names like Lame, Quinn, Kelly, Tommie. We found notes that they would sit

My mother's parents on their wedding day, Jim Moroney and Rosie Wimmers.

around and talk of "the good times we used to be having when we worked on the gravel train," laying the gravel on the railbed.

In the last few years I finally got around to visiting this cemetery, which is only about 15 miles southwest of Elyria. I found the Moroney tombstones on the left side near the entrance. Most were faded and hard to read, but it was a thrill to find them and I go back frequently now.

Dennis, who was the father of grandfather Jim, and Dennis had a brother, Patrick, who came from Limerick, Ireland, and settled near Bucyrus, Ohio, 60 miles from Elyria. Neither knew where the other had gone when they came to the U.S. until Patrick put an ad in the Catholic newspaper, the Boston Pilot, seeking his brother. He found him near Kipton. The Bucyrus Patrick Moroney then moved to a farm next door to his brother Dennis, my great grandfather, in Kipton. This is still rural farmland in Ohio but most of the Irish have moved into Cleveland or Elyria. The West Side of Cleveland still has a large Irish settlement.

The Moroneys in Limerick, Ireland, originally spelled their name in Gaelic, O'Maornaridhs. They were of Milesian stock, which means they were part of the Spanish who sailed up and took over part of Ireland. The name Milesian comes from the name of the Spanish King who led this invasion, Ir Miled. His name also led to the word Ireland. The people living in Ireland in the Fifth and Sixth century when the Spanish came were Danish and Anglo Saxon, which means they were British and German. The Danish part was called Norman, or Scandinavian.

No one has traced the origin of the Moroney family from these earlier peoples.

Spiritually the Irish added an element of laughter and joy so that I have usually been able to see the humor in any situation. It kept me from getting too serious, even in bad times.

The tiny woman Grandfather Jim married, Rosalee Wimmers, had a German history. Rosalee's father (my great grandfather) was Hubert Wimmers, and his father was Godfred Wimmers (my great, great grandfather).

Hubert's wife was Mary Kristlemeier, also German, and

they lived in Elyria with their children, Rosalee, who became my grandmother, and Annie, Lizzie, Mary, Sam, and Johnnie. I can recall my great aunts Annie and Mary. Aunt Mary lived with us almost until her death at 93.

I have many good memories of Aunt Mary. She was proud of her German background and had countless stories to tell about growing up in Elyria. She was born on Christmas day when the Civil War ended. Lincoln was President. She seemed like a chapter out of history to me. She remembered the first cars in Elyria, the mud streets, the wooden bridges over the two Black Rivers.

She said her rosary every day and read from a worn book of prayers for hours. At Christmas she would drink a few small glasses of brandy and then demonstrate how she could still touch her toes without a bend of the knee. Soon after this Christmas ritual Aunt Mary would fall asleep. The last months of her life she went to a nursing home and died there peacefully.

Aunt Annie married Will Smith and they had Smith's Grocery Store in Elyria, formerly at the corner of West River and Lodi, where the trolley turned around after coming from the steel mill in Lorain. It turned around and headed back to the mill. Many of the Elyria men cashed their paycheck at Smiths, and bought groceries. Aunt Annie had six children, including one who became Sister Mary Michella, a Mother Superior in the Cleveland Notre Dame nuns.

Aunt Annie was part of my growing up too. The grocery store was sold but Aunt Annie and her daughter Margaret ran a candy and "notions" store next door. Margaret was completely deaf and I often helped her in the store after school. The bare wooden floors were always clean, and there was a high ladder that moved along each side wall on tracks to get the high items. I loved to work on that ladder.

Arnold, a son of Aunt Annie, would drive out to our home in the country with his mother and Margaret every Sunday afternoon in their immense black car, a Falcon Knight. Their arrival was a highlight of the day for me since I got to sit in the car while they visited my parents. Aunt Annie was tiny, like her sister Rosalee I was told, and very prim and proper. Once

This is an old tintype taken about 1860 showing great grandpa Hubert Wimmers and grandma Mary Wimmers (Kristlemeier). Their children were great aunts and uncles, Johnie, Annie (Smith) Mary, Sam, Francis, and Lizzie. Rosie, my mother's mother was yet to come. Hubert was one of Godfred's and Eva's sons, and they came from Germany to southern Ohio. Hubert was a tailor in Elyria.

some Cleveland friends of my parents were visiting on a Sunday and a "city" woman in the family made the mistake of offering Aunt Annie a cigarette. She drew herself up to a proper stiffness and told the woman she did not smoke and that they were leaving. They left as Arnold and Margaret marched to the car behind Aunt Annie, leaving behind an indignant "city" woman.

Aunt Annie and the others lived in an apartment over their old store, operated by other people in my times. The house was Victorian in decor with furniture that seemed delicate and was covered with lace doilies. I almost hated to sit on any chair, and felt like I was in a museum. Aunt Annie died after a long sickness and I had seen her just a few days before her death. I remember telling her it was alright to go ahead and die. She had been hanging on so long.

Sister Michella was another tiny woman. She was a Notre Dame sister as long as I knew her and she visited us once or twice a year. She would sip a little wine after saying she shouldn't. When she grew older we visited her in the convent and always enjoyed her gentle ways. We went to her funeral and were with a big gathering of several hundred nuns of all ages.

My great-grandfather Hubert ran the Wimmers' Tailor Shop at 82 Broad St. in Elyria all his life. Great "Uncle Johnny" had the Midget Candy Store in front of their home at 965 East River, a few blocks from where we live now. The home still looks about the same except a new house sits on the part of the lot where the candy store was located, and the double grape arbor leading to the front door is gone.

The house built by Hubert Wimmers at 965 East River in Elyria. My mother and father were borders here. The little Midget Store is on the right. Aunt Lizzie and Aunt Mary, left to right, and Jim Lucas, my cousin, to my right.

The Midget Store is part of my childhood memory. It was a very small building, I think about 40 feet by 40, packed with gum and candy, the penny kind. I would go in there and be overwhelmed, but I was too small to help out.

My mother had one sister, my Aunt Agnes. Agnes spends the last years of her life battling cancer. Before that she had been married to Russell Lucas and they had a plumbing company in Elyria. I remember Russell as a playful man but he was sick a long time and died, and I did not know him well. Aunt Agnes worked as a secretary to an attorney in Elyria, who became a prosecutor in the county, and later she became an auditor for the Ohio Turnpike. They had a son, my cousin Jim, and we played together in our younger days. He became a NASA engineer and lives in Elyria.

My mother was four years older than her sister. Like their own mother, Rosalee, Katie was small. She had a warm and jovial personality and a great love for life. Her real name was Catherine Moroney, but everyone called her Katie. As a child she learned to play the violin from her fiddle-playing father.

She attended St. Mary's school in Elyria, the same building where I later went. She went to Elyria High School from which I also graduated. Then her mother, Rosalee, died and her father soon remarried. As a young woman Katie's first big job was at the Cleveland Trust Bank in that city. She rode the street car back and forth, the same line on which her father was conductor. She loved that job and the big city and the friends she made, with some remaining close all her life.

In her late twenties her father Jim also died and she moved in with the Wimmers family, in the wooden house on East River, built by Grandpa Hubert. The same house where my father became a boarder.

My main source of information on my Irish side over the years was my mother. She had a hundred pictures of the relatives and collected written memories from any people she could find. She loved to tell her Irish stories in an Irish brogue and knew some Gaelic phrases. She turned 93 in 1990.

Hubert Wimmers, my grandfather, and his four brothers were brought to this country when he was eight, by Godfred and his wife, Eva. They came from Gasweiler, Dusseldorf,

Prussia. Godfred was disowned by his family in Prussia because he married a French foundling. Some of the French foundlings were Jewish babies from the persecuted Ashkenazi Communities of Alsace-Lorraine. These Jews were called "Ashkenazim," meaning German.

Godfred's Catholic parents were ragpickers and poor, and we think they disowned Godfred because he married a French foundling Jewish woman. He would not have been disowned for marrying below his state in life, as a ragpicker was so low. That left relatives to believe the reason for being disowned was his Jewish wife.

At that time Napoleon was in power. In 1807 he made Paris the center of French Jewry and built many synagogues. Napoleon started Paris on the Ile De La Cite in the middle of the Seine, where the Cathedral of Notre Dame is now. The main street was called Jewry Street and is still lined with Jewish shops. Great-great-grandfather Godfred sided with Napoleon, which adds to the belief that his wife was Jewish, since Napoleon favored Jews to some extent.

Godfred brought his family to Cincinnati, and then to Minster, Ohio, near the German Maria Stein Shrine and Lake St. Mary's by Indiana. From there Hubert came to Elyria, but no one knows why. All the rest of the Wimmers clan stayed in Southwestern Ohio in the town of St. Henry, near Minster.

In the year of my trial Mary and I visited this area of Ohio for the first time and had a great day looking up dead and live relatives.

If the Irish gave me a sense of joy and laughter, perhaps the German side gave me determination to organize things, including my religion and my spiritual life. I like things to be in order.

Prayer

"O Lord, thank you for letting me know about the people of my ancestry. It is one of the great mysteries of life how each of us is born in our particular circumstances, out of all the millions of possibilities. My Irish and German families helped make me what I am. This has given me many pleasures in thinking about the wit of the Irish, the industry of the Germans, and the strong Catholic faith of both.

"Help me to always appreciate my relatives."

Chapter 5

The Protestant Side of my Family: Peters and Huntley

I have some information on the family of my father's mother and a lot on the Peters side. We trace every relative on father's side back to Thomas Dunwood Petters, born in 1550 in Fowey Parish, England. We found the identical history in three different sources.

One was the diary of Congressman William A. Ashbrook from Ohio, now deceased. The Ashbrook and Peters clans lived on Ohio farms near one another and started marrying in the late 1700s.

Clara Peters Horn died in 1960 in Columbus, Ohio and also kept family records in detail and knew many relatives. Finally, Mary and I found a book in a store in St. Johns, New Brunswick, Canada on the American Loyalists, and there was more history of the Peters's.

The Loyalists were Americans who were loyal to the King of England in the Revolution and fled to Canada. We found out about this whole part of the family by accident in that bookstore. No one knew what happened to John Peters and his people. They were called Tories by the "Rebels."

John got a degree from Yale in 1759 but fought on the side of the king in the Revolution, going to jail and later fighting his father who was a Colonel in the service of America. Then he escaped to Montreal.

On my father's mother's side were the Huntleys, my middle name. My grandmother, Hattie Belle Huntley was born in 1885, died in 1917, having two children, my father, and Ralph

My father as a baby with his parents, Clyde Peters and Hattie Huntley Peters. They died of TB when he was a child, so I never knew them.

Malcolm Peters, who died at age one. My grandmother died when she was 31, her husband at 27, so at age 9 my father was an orphan.

The Huntleys were from Cheraw, South Carolina: Huntley Furniture, Huntley Used Cars, and a big farm, complete with former slaves in log cabins. I spent a day watching these former slaves on the tobacco farm and saw their neat row of wooden cabins. That was in the early 1950s and they still seemed like slaves to me.

My father was sent to an aunt in Columbus on Chittenden Avenue, near Ohio State University, at age 12. This aunt, Clara Horn, was one of the collectors of this history.

At 14 father came to other aunts in Elyria, one a Mate Huntley Koehle, and got to know Jack Drage, a local Elyria policeman married to his Giede relatives. My father made friends with the Wimmers family on East River, and as a young adult moved in there with two other partial orphans, Katie and Agnes Moroney, related to the Wimmers's.

He courted and married Katie and they lived there; Agnes married Russell Lucas and they built a house at 138 Denison, around the corner. I used to play there all the time. My father became a Catholic at marriage.

From the Peters history: Dunwood, born in England in 1550, had two sons, Ezra and Hugh. Hugh was a follower of Cromwell and a judge who condemned to death King Charles I, and then donned the executioner's garb to cut off his head. Later Hugh was executed and his head placed on London Bridge. This is in a book "The Day They Killed the King." Congressman Ashbrook traced this also.

I found a book called "Oliver Cromwell" by John Buchanan with many references to Hugh Peters, who supported Cromwell and was the judge and executioner of King Charles I. Hugh, a minister, was himself beheaded at Charing Cross in 1660. This is a main stop on the London subway, known to all Londoners, and remembered well by Mary and I from a trip there.

Hugh came to America, according to Ashbrook's records, but went back to England after living with nephews here. His brother Ezra stayed here and started the Peters clan.

This Ezra Petters came to America in 1607 at 17, to Jamestown, Virginia, near Williamsburg. He went to New England and with others started Harvard and Yale. His sons went to Pennsylvania and New York. The name was changed to Peters. Ezra's son Newton was born in 1655, Newton's son Absolom in 1703, his son Zachariah in Virginia in 1730. He married a girl from Holland whose last name was Harrison and they had five children, including my great, great, great grandfather, Tunis. He married Francina Adams, cousin of John Adams, second President of the new country, the United States. They had 13 children, one my great, great grandfather Elder Mahlon Peters, born in 1791. They had Myron, and he had Clyde, my grandfather, who married the Huntley girl, Belle. In 1989 Mary and I found some of their burial places on a memorable trip during my trial.

Myron Peters married Caroline Light, whom he met in Lightsville, in Southwest Ohio. This is about 25 miles from the territory of the Wimmers relatives in Minster, Ohio. That's Hubert Wimmers who moved to Elyria, my maternal grandfather.

Here is what it looks like when I write out the list of my grandfathers on my father's side: Great 9x Grandfather Dunwood, born in 1550. He stayed in England and had sons Ezra and Hugh, Ezra was my 8x grandfather, born in 1590. Then Newton, 7x, 1655, born in America. Absolom, 6x, 1703. Zachariah Peters, 5x, 1730. Tunis, 4x, 1749. Mahlon 3x, 1791. James Peters, my great great grandfather, born 1821. Myron, great grandfather, 1845. Clyde, my grandfather, my father's father, born 1881 and my father, Harrison Huntley Peters, born Oct. 12, 1907.

Great grandfather Myron was born near Galloway, Ohio, on the Lavely farm and at 17 went into the army in the Civil War. He was one of the bodyguards for Abraham Lincoln when he lay in state in Columbus, Ohio, on the way home for burial. Myron died at age 88, the last man in Company D, 88th. Regiment, to die.

My father, Harrison Huntley Peters, is a tall man, over six feet, and as I grow older I look like him. He was always interested in building and making things, and as he grew older and had spare time he took up hobbies of raising flowers, especially hybrid lilies. Before that he had goats, bees, and several ducks, a pig, a cow, and many chickens. He still has a wonderful vegetable garden. He has sweet corn all summer, peas, beans, lettuce, cabbage, tomatoes, beets, onions, cauliflower, celery, leeks, parsley, asparagus, and dill. There are strawberries, raspberries, blueberries, elderberries, plums, apples, and pears. What he doesn't can or freeze, he gives away, and has done so for years.

My father likes to discuss any subject at hand, and can argue either side of an issue. I avoid arguments to keep peace. He has been involved in his parish council and parish affairs all his life. He writes letters about lilies to people all over the United States and other countries, and keeps up with the latest lists and developments, being active in the American Lily Society.

Pete worries about the health of my mother and greatly misses talking and joking with her. It is hard to face that these happy times seem to be gone. Their life has been filled with

Taken at the 60th wedding anniversary of my parents. A party in the basement of Sacred Heart Church in Elyria.

friends, especially younger ones as they grew older. Many came to their country place, New Havoc, to enjoy Pete and Katie and share a pot of soup and some homemade bread, with a cherry or elderberry pie.

What do I get spiritually from my father's side of the family? I think it is a sense of rootedness, of belonging, and also of the earth, of what it produces. We lived off the land.

We can trace our history back a long time, including an important part of this country and Canada. Perhaps there is also a genteel element, a refined, educated, cultured part that comes from the English. There are connections to the southern part of the United States and the involvement with black people and slavery.

Prayer

"O Lord, I also appreciate the English side of my family. They were some of the first European people to come to this land. They mixed with the Indians who had come earlier from Siberia, and were later joined by the people from all parts of the world who moved to America. I look forward to meeting all my family in the next life."

Chapter 6

Marriage, Birth, and Early Schooling

Harrison and Catherine got to know each other when they lived in the Wimmers' boarding house. Before that my father was living with those different aunts in Elyria and in his early 20's he went to Canada to find work. He got a job in Kerrobert, Saskatchewan, in the harvest fields, near Moosejaw. Absence made the hearts grow fonder and when he returned, love bloomed between Pete and Katie. On Feb 22, 1928 they got married in a simple ceremony at St Mary's Church in Elyria. My father had become a Catholic to marry my mother, but this wasn't too difficult. Despite the strong Baptist background he had no church affiliation because of moving around with so many different relatives.

My father was now a surveyor for a private company in Elyria, but soon after marriage he began to work for the Lorain County Engineer's Department.

As a young married couple, they continued to live at the Wimmers's and soon my mother became pregnant. I was born on March 29, 1929, a very red-faced, pinched headed ugly baby.

They said one side of my head was dented from birth problems; I still see that feature when I look in the mirror.

It was Good Friday, a half hour before the marking of the death of Jesus, when I came into this world.

I have always tried to see the spiritual significance of the events in my life, how they tie in with religious feasts and seasons. Things do not happen by chance, in my view.

I was arrested in 1988 on the legal charges and went to the local jail for booking on the Feast of the Holy Innocents, Dec. 28. This was always a feast I liked. It honors the infants killed by King Herod in his attempt to kill the baby the three kings told him about.

Being born on Good Friday has always been significant to me. Suffering, physical and mental, is part of life. Coming into this world at the time in the liturgical year when the church is re-enacting the death moments of Christ has meaning.

The liturgy of Good Friday is the most heart-rending of the entire year, and strong feelings come at that time of the afternoon as a choir chants the "reproaches," in which Christ asks "his people" why they are killing him. What had he done to them? He fed them with manna, they gave him gall and vinegar. "Oh my people, what have I done to you?"

I was a sickly baby at birth. I would not eat or sleep properly and after some weeks it looked like I might not live. My parents called in Father John Schaffeld, the German pastor from St. Mary's and he came to our house intending to baptize me. My parents gave me to him to hold.

I was crying and red-faced as usual. In a little while I stopped crying, the first time in days. The priest stayed a long time, holding me, and I fell asleep, to everyone's surprise. The priest put me in my crib and left without baptizing me, not wanting to disturb my much needed sleep.

I woke after a long time, ate normally, and was not a sick baby anymore. My parents took it to be a miracle. Although I was not aware of any of this, I now know about it from their stories and it helps me see that God has a plan and a concern for me. This increases my desire to place my trust in him. The Lord who took care of me then has taken care of me ever since.

The city of Elyria had a new resident, Thomas Huntley Peters. Elyria is an industrial city on two rivers, called the Black River, the East Branch and the West Branch, joining together in the downtown of the city. The waters drop over two different falls and then become one river to flow 10 miles through Lorain and into Lake Erie.

Elyria was settled by landowners from Connecticut, Heman Ely, and his family. They remained here because of the rivers, a means of transportation and power for grinding grain. The waterfalls drop into a rugged area in the heart of downtown called Cascade Park, where the water cascades down into the valley formed by the retreating glaciers, leaving caves and boulders. Every kid in Elyria plays and climbs there and sleds down the hills in the winter. The name "Black River" comes from the black chestnut trees once found along the banks.

The city of Elyria became the county seat, although Lorain was bigger. My trial took place in the courtrooms on the square in my hometown.

I grew from babyhood to school age in Elyria, with aunts and a few uncles taking care of me in that house on the river. They tell me I had a small garden, and once went around the neighborhood trying to sell a quart of beans for $50. I never sold any, but told my family I would be rich if I could sell only one quart.

The early years of school at St. Mary's are not memorable.

A photo of me at age 3 taken by Charles Scheide, the chief photographer of all Elyria, and our next door neighbor on East River. The background was the Scheide garden.

That same old brick building where my mother went to school had three floors and a black iron fire escape which terrified me. We had fire drills during which we would go out the third floor exit and down to the ground.

In the third grade I had my first encounter with the mysterious. My classroom was on the second floor then and the one directly above us was empty, but had a small pump organ. Every once in a while we would hear music from above and the sister teaching us finally selected me and two others to sneak up and see who was playing it and distracting us.

One day the music was playing and we went up carefully, fearfully. No one was in there. It had to be a ghost. To this day I have dreams about that school building and the stairway, and do not know what to make of that music. In my dreams I am usually wandering around in the building, trying to get out, or wandering around in the playground.

When I was in the third grade, my father completed work on a small home he had been building on five acres four miles outside Elyria. He and Katie bought this land when I was born. They read a book entitled *Five Acres and Independence* and decided to have just that.

My father had never built anything like a house, so he used books and the advice of friends. Before trying to erect the house, he built a shed to hold the goats. He planted fruit trees, apples, peaches, plums, pears, put out bee hives, and followed the plan in *Five Acres and Independence*.

When I was at the end of the third grade we made the move into the mostly completed house. I began my life in the country, riding the big yellow school bus twice a day from then through high school. It came at 7:20 every morning except in the deepest snow, when it was late. On some glorious days it never came at all.

One day a boy in the back of the bus (riders worked their way back, from the youngest in front to the oldest in school having command of the back seats) fired a spitball at the bus driver, a heavy set farmer, whose name was Irving. The driver put the culprit out to walk home. I wrote an essay about this and it was published in the Elyria Chronicle Telegram. I was a seventh grader at the time and when Irving read it, he also put me off the bus for making him look bad. That was my first newspaper article and we still have it, in one of the many scrap books collected by my mother.

At first, in addition to goats and chickens, we had a big garden with all those vegetables, a few ducks, a scottie dog, then a "wiener dog," cats, and gerbils. All the pets had unusual names. One duck was Lord Chesterfield; he was very regal and had a strange following of some lady ducks of a different color, shape, and breed.

Dogs were Daffy and Schnitzel, and they looked and behaved like their name. Somewhere in those early days, the Peters' country place got named New Havoc, because something was always being built: a new room on the house, an indoor toilet, a basement, another well. There were always new animals. And new company visited often. Many were friends from Cleveland.

My parents started a literary club, called The Hasty Pudding Club, which attracted more visitors. Mother joined the Women's Christian Temperance Union, the only club on the road in this rural area. She called it WICTU. It was the only way to meet the neighbor women. Later I recall a group called the "Ladies Aid Society" and Katie went to that also.

When I was 5, long before the New Havoc days, a brother, David was born. When we moved to the country, we played together since there were only a few other kids around.

I made friends with the neighbor farmers, people named Walkers, who had Brown Swiss cattle, which are still my favorites to see at county fairs. I learned to milk them by hand, to get around their stubborn ways, to be nice to the bull, and to love the smell of barnyard cow manure. I still love that smell.

Mrs. Oma Walker took care of us when my parents worked. By now my mother was a secretary in the music department at Oberlin College, my father custodian of some of the buildings there. Mrs. Walker made wonderful cookies to keep my brother and I happy.

My memories of religion in grade school: I had to go to Mass every morning and had to sit and kneel up straight. A nun would frown and whisper when I slouched down, leaning my bottom against the seat, a much more comfortable position.

Our family. My brother Dave on the left, me on the right. I was 5 years older than Dave.

Church was like the bus, with the youngest sitting in front, I guess so they could see, and the eighth graders sitting in back, privileged, able to get away with more whispering and slouching down.

I did not understand the Mass, the Liturgy, but I liked the sound and the sight and the smell. I can still hear the sounds of Gregorian Chant and the real organ. A woman did the singing, but it sounded churchly. The incense smelled good. The vestments, especially the gold ones, looked godlike and fit for rituals, the movements of most priests were slow and majestic. I was never an altar boy because I lived in the country, and I also felt I could never learn the Latin and the moves.

The hymns, now mostly considered old fashioned, also grew on me: hymns to Mary, to the Sacred Heart of Jesus, to the Trinity. They were slow, had a predictable pace and easy words. My favorite was a hymn usually used in the Benediction

New Havoc, the home my father built, on West Ridge outside Elyria.

ceremony honoring the Eucharist, the hymn *"Pange Lingua," Sing My Tongue the Savior's Glory*. Later I learned this was written by St. Thomas Aquinas and sung to a melody used in the times of Caesar, a marching song. I still love that song.

The church itself, St. Mary's, in downtown Elyria, is a typical late 1800 German Gothic American brick structure. Back then it had lots of statues, candles, fancy wooden carvings, busy stained glass windows, hard, straight backed wooden pews, and a nice bell tower and bell, which I loved to hear calling people to worship or marking the time. I have always loved bells.

Now the Church has been modernized and is very plain. Back then it seemed more devotional for me.

The second sickness came along for me. In the eighth grade I developed tuberculosis and left school for a year. Both of my father's parents died of this when they were young. Today the disease is treated with chemotherapy, but when I had it in

1942, the cure was rest and a good diet. Rest meant lots of sleep and lots of sitting around other times. I learned to love to read that year; the Rover Boys, the Hardy Boys, and other adventure books. Reading filled hours and hours. I loved Pecos Bill, a Paul Bunyon type cowboy, tall tales. Learning to really enjoy reading was a very big thing in my life. It still is.

I repeated the eighth grade at St. Mary's but have few memories. I had to get used to a new set of classmates as the old ones, with me all through elementary school, had gone on to high school that year.

Our eighth grade teacher told us to bid farewell to one another because the large high school would destroy our friendships and we would be scattered about.

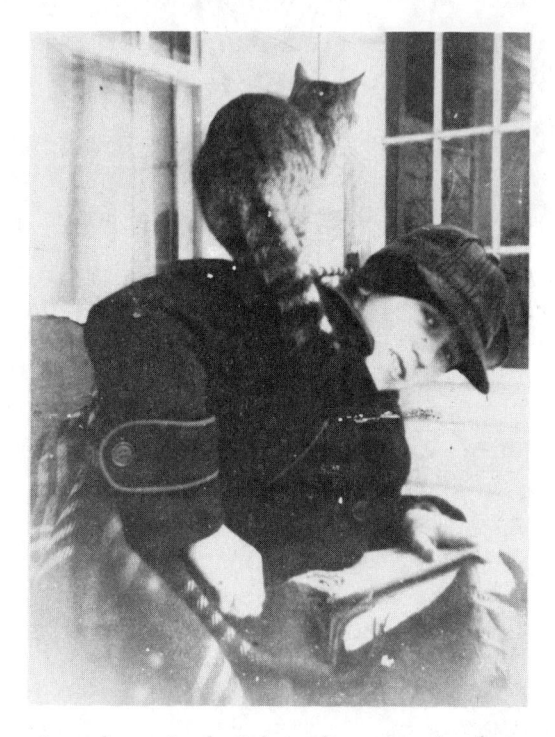

I was home in the 8th grade, recovering from TB, learning to love reading, and dealing with the New Havoc cat, Zany. My favorite book was Pecos Bill.

Prayer

"How can I understand the great wonder of my birth to a man and woman who met in Elyria, fell in love, married, and conceived me. There was the further great wonder of my staying alive.

"O Lord, you had a priest enter my life, a newborn infant, part of my restoration to health. You watched over me like the angels watched over the infant Jesus. My parents presented me to our parish priest like Jesus was presented to Simeon.

"Thank you for taking care of me."

Chapter 7

High school, Forest View Farm, and Oberlin

As I entered high school, my world began to expand. Elyria High School was my first public school. I spent four years there, ending as editor of the school paper, The Herald. I challenged the administration on some policies and began a life-long combative attitude for "causes" and what I perceived as unfair authority, and authority figures. I was a rebel.

During these years, two priests who influenced me a lot entered my life. They were Monsignor William Newton, and Father Charles Hogan. Msgr. Newton came to St. Mary's as pastor with a doctoral degree in Sacred Scripture, one of the few priests with a Doctorate in the United States. He taught in the seminary in Cleveland and at Catholic University in Washington, D. C. and organized an international association of Catholic biblical scholars. He was involved in translating the New Testament into modern English called the Confraternity Version. Newton had been raised in the tough Irish area of downtown Cleveland called The Angle, near the Cuyahoga River. In his seminary studies he was so exceptional that he was sent to Rome for the scripture degrees. He also became an excellent golfer and a lover of mystery stories.

For various reasons he wanted a parish and less of the scholar role, which was often filled with bitter arguments over

Monsignor William L. Newton who was my guide in life, in high school, the seminary twice, and the Cursillo and marriage.

translations of words, petty scholarly detail and viewpoints, and schools of thought.

Father Hogan was different. He had played piano with Fred Waring in his younger days, was active nationally in the labor movement, and had a drinking problem and other difficulties. He came to St. Mary's as a refuge, knowing Msgr. Newton would take him in. He was short, balding, and had a smiling happy appearance.

Both priests liked causes: minorities, poor people, working people. Both were intellectual and well-read, and had world views, rather than narrow, parochial ones. Monsignor's initial influence was to make me want to hear him talk about biblical times, revealing the history behind so many events, making it alive. Father Hogan told me to stick up for my religion in school when people made fun of me for being a Catholic. The students who were Catholic joined together and in our senior year we scored a small world triumph by electing Father Hogan as the minister to speak before graduation. He was the first priest to do so in that school, which opened in 1850, and this was 1948. I was active in this event.

The Catholic Church, and religion, entered my life in another way as I left grade school. About a mile from our New Havoc country home was a big farm belonging to the Sisters of Charity of St. Augustine. It was given to them by a wealthy, aristocratic man who kept it for fun, raising purebred animals. He liked the sisters because they ran Parmadale, an orphanage in Cleveland, and some hospitals. I thought he may have lived in that orphanage. Parmadale and these Sisters of Charity became part of my social work life later.

The sisters used this farm as a retirement center for nuns, who lived in the big house, complete with chapel. Priests who had alcohol problems lived in a small house nearby. They were supposed to be cured in the country air. Farmhands lived in a third house and took care of the animals and raised food for the sisters' establishments in Cleveland.

I started going there to help out, especially at thrashing time, enjoying the big gatherings of area farmers and the immense tables of food prepared by the nuns. In time I got to know some of the priests living in the small house near the big one. I would serve Mass in the chapel, which held about 20 people, most of whom were the nuns.

One priest had a beautiful Irish Setter which always sat on the altar steps during Mass, quietly watching. I learned a lesson in this, that animals can be part of sacred things if people don't get upset and cause a fuss. Later in the seminary I did a lot of reading on the "souls" of animals and what happens when pets die. I think a beloved pet will have a place in our eternity. That priest was inseparable from his dog, and would not be completely himself without it. In heaven we will be fully ourselves.

One of these priests changed my views of the sacrament of confession. I would see him in his house and tell him I wanted to go to confession. He would offer me some candy and sit down in his easy chair. He told me to sit or to kneel, then to tell him what I wished to confess. Then he gave me penance, words of wisdom, absolution, and we would just sit and talk after it was over. The screened separation between priest and penitent did not exist.

I also came to see nuns in a different light than in school. At the farm they were more relaxed, more at peace, more tolerant of mistakes. The very older ones were usually named for their task, so there was Sister Chicken, Sister Vegetables, Sister Garden. Their domain was in their name. I liked Sister Chicken the most.

Forest View Farm was a beautiful place, with hills, meadows, wandering cows, a river, fences to climb, big horses, the smell of silage and fresh cut hay, dusty straw, and a haymow high in the biggest barn I had ever seen.

I liked that quiet chapel, too. I used to sit or kneel there alone, with no special thoughts except that this place was some kind of mystery and had a connection with God, the supernatural. I spent many hours, usually alone, along the Black River flowing through this property. I played in the mud, made buildings, watched the cows drinking, and threw stones into the water.

During these years I also got to know Oberlin College, with both my parents working there. Sometimes they would take me along to work in the summer months, or my father would take me on weekends when something special was going on. He was custodian in the small building where the president of the college had offices and I could sit at his desk if I wanted. I would check out the women's restrooms for my father to be sure they were empty before he cleaned them. I never found anyone on these ventures into forbidden territories.

My favorite building where he cleaned was Finney Chapel, where the concerts and recitals were all held, and where famous lecturers spoke. It is still there and looks the same, with a wonderful pipe organ as the focal point above and in back of the stage.

For all Finney Chapel events, my father would run the microphones and speaker system, and my mother would often be backstage to help people find the rest rooms and dressing rooms. She would go for forgotten essentials, like icewater, or mouthwash.

I would help out some, but mostly just enjoy the rehearsal or the event and the crowds. My parents would take home programs signed by the famous, like Rachmaninoff, Marian Anderson, Eleanor Roosevelt, Paul Robeson, and Ezio Pinza. I held Eleanor Roosevelt's dog at a noon speech while my father tried to lower the First Lady's high pitched, squeaky voice on the amplifier. The dog was not the famous Fala, but a small French poodle which traveled with her.

I got to climb around inside the organ as my father cleaned it, and heard hours and hours of students and faculty practicing Bach and Vivaldi, still my favorite music. I heard the Cleveland Orchestra and many others. I often stood in the wings off stage, enjoying the sounds which could be picked out from the kettle drums, the violins, the bass.

Those years filled me with a love for the kind of classical music that is controlled and ordered, like Bach, but I never did enjoy much of the modern experimental music which still seems noisy and going nowhere, like Bartok and even Stravinski.

Oberlin did not influence my religious life directly, but I found music to be meditative, restful, an opening to thinking about God. I started to find architecture interesting in some of the older buildings on the campus, like the Carnegie Library, Peters Hall (no relation), the theology school buildings, the Allen Museum of Art. Good architecture is very spiritual for me whether it is a church (Notre Dame in Paris is my favorite), a skyscraper or a house.

By the time I was ending high school I also learned to have an easy relationship with priests at St. Mary's and at Forest View Farm. At the farm I would now regularly sit down in the living room of their house, munch on candy, pet the dog, and make my confession.

One couple, Larry and Betty Davis, began to have a special influence on me in high school in my religion and my spiritual life. He was a Lorain County court reporter and they lived across from St. Mary's. I would stay there some nights when I did not want to go back to the country.

Larry had shelves and shelves of books in the living room and dining room, on theology, philosophy, history, English writers like Chesterton, Belloc, classic novels, some books in Latin, German, French. When not working or talking, Larry would be reading. He also prayed the Breviary, now called the Liturgy of the Hours, in Latin every day, and went to daily morning Mass. He was an intellectual, a college professor, working as a court reporter in little Elyria.

His job also meant a wide variety of people went in and out of their house, seeking transcripts of trials and hearings immediately, at once. A court reporter is the person who writes or types everything down as it happens in a legal event, and then makes copies for all who want them and for the court record. In those days Larry and everyone else wrote in shorthand, so it was quite a skill. Larry eventually lost his hearing and retired out West.

One of the things I learned from Larry was an increased love for books and learning. I have hundreds of books now and can spend hours in bookstores and libraries. Larry Davis knew every book in his house and where it was located.

Near the end of my high school year, there was a near-death event in my life. I was riding in the front seat of a car, next to the driver, on the way to Bowling Green, Ohio, where others in the car were going to check out the University there. The car we were in hit a patch of ice or water and overturned in a roadside ditch. I was bruised and some were seriously hurt so we all went to the hospital. When we later went to see the car, the roof was below the glove compartment where I had been sitting. The lack of seat belts caused me to be thrown under the dash, saving my life.

Again, the Lord seemed to be watching over me. I scarcely realized it though.

Prayer

"My teen years passed so fast. I was a town boy and a country boy, trying to find my direction in life.

"Lord, you were already leading me along the path of my lifelong interest in religion, the spiritual side of things, and the joy of reading and learning. This all came through the sisters and priests at Forest View Farm, Oberlin College, and the Davis's house.

"Thank you for those teen years."

Chapter 8

Dayton, a Cemetery, Death

The summer of 1948 I worked in a shoe store in downtown Elyria and prepared for my first year in college. I had been accepted at the University of Dayton and would be studying for a bachelor of arts degree. I signed up for history and english, speech, journalism, and needing something in science, geology, and Spanish. By now I really liked journalism and was assigned to write sports articles for the school paper, The Flyer. But geology turned out to be my favorite subject, although I had never liked science or math. We learned about rocks and the formation of the earth and I came to know what made up the part of the world I was in. This has interested me all my life.

Dayton was operated by the brothers and priests of the Society of Mary community, usually called The Marianists. This was my first acquaintance with brothers, and with men living in a community.

My mind began to think about the relationships between science and religion, the question of the existence of God. My future. What would I be?

The campus chapel was a small building holding several hundred. It was brick with an ornate appearance inside, lots of gold trim. Students could walk between classes by cutting through the chapel building, or walk around it. I often found myself going into the mostly empty chapel to enjoy the silence, the gold, the moment apart. I didn't know why I liked it.

I lived in various private houses off campus with other students, remembering best two soft-spoken boys from Kentucky who were my first contact with Southerners. One met and married an Elyria girl, a friend of mine, and we stay in touch. The other went to work for the University of Dayton administration and is still there. We ate meals at the big cafeteria at the National Cash Register plant, giving me one of the few contacts in my life with factory workers. We "passed" as workers in the food line.

Toward the end of my freshman year I was on my way home for lunch one day, climbing the steep hill in the local cemetery, a shortcut I usually took home. I got a terrible pain in the left chest, fell to the ground on a tombstone, and could not move or breathe.

When I tried to get up the pain was greater, my breath shorter. In a panic I crawled to the cemetery drive and laid there. Two older people came along in a car and I waved for help. They probably thought I was drunk or mentally ill. The Dayton Psychiatric Institute was on one side of the cemetery, the university on the other.

They gave me a ride to the gate of the cemetery with me laying on the rear floor of their car. I somehow crawled the block to my rooming house and the landlady, a motherly woman, called an ambulance.

Laying flat on the stretcher I could breathe a little and the pain was less but I had no idea what was wrong as I went to the hospital. It turned out to be a spontaneous pneumo thorax, a collapsed left lung. The lung lining had torn loose from my rib cage from the strain of the climb up the hill. Apparently I was overly tired or exhausted. When I breathed, the air went through the torn area between the lung and the heart instead of into the lung, thus pushing against the heart, causing the terrible pain.

I was put in an oxygen tent and told not to move. A priest came to give me the last rites of the Catholic church, my parents arrived from Elyria and I looked pretty sick. Again.

I could not do anything for myself. I was fed, wiped, had my nose blown, everything. When those things weren't going on, I was in the oxygen tent. This was a clear plastic tent-like structure covering the body, fastened to an oxygen tank. This gave me air to keep me from having to breathe myself, so the lung could heal itself and seal itself back to normal.

After a few weeks in the Dayton hospital the school said they would give me credit for the year without exams, since I had done well in class, and the doctors said I should go home to Elyria, but flat on a stretcher.

The cheapest way to do that was by train, so one day an ambulance took me to the train station and I was lifted up in the air and put through a train window and into a bed, getting off in Wellington, Ohio, the same way, and going home by "Benny Bittner" the Elyria ambulance and funeral home used by Catholics. One of my "handlers" was Johnnie Wirscham, husband of Gert Wirscham, who later opened and ran Betterway's Search Shop after her husband died. She is still there at age 73 in 1990.

Back home at New Havoc I could move around a little but it was about the same as when I had TB six years earlier. I mostly had to lay around.

Father Charles Hogan started to visit me almost daily. He did not drive, so he would arrive at New Havoc by cab and leave a few hours later the same way, a 10 mile round trip.

He brought me a little psalm book by a Father Frey, published by the Confraternity, the people who were doing Msgr. Newton's bible. The psalm book was arranged for the seven days of the week according to monastic hours and illustrated with engravings. It contained small, powerful drawings by an artist, Ariel Agemian, who worked three years to make this first complete illustrated edition of the new translation of the psalms.

I learned about God, about the Lord, Yahweh. I read the psalms for hours and God became personal: loving, creating, judging, calling, punishing, banishing, eternal, always was and always will be. I had never known God this way.

Next Father Hogan gave me a New Testament, illustrated by the same artist, partly translated by Monsignor Newton. I met Christ. He was a person, a human being, he really lived.

He loved, prayed the psalms, loved God his father, loved people, was rejected by his friends, suffered, died, rose again, still lives on.

I could not believe what I was finding out, and I remember reading or praying aloud, and crying sometimes over the beauty of the words and ideas. This was my conversion to adult religion.

There was one more book that summer, the life of a priest in France, St. John Vianney, called the Cure de Ars, the priest of the small city of Ars, France. This long book was the first biography I had ever read. In this book I met a priest who listened to people who came to him from all over France and Europe to talk about their problems and go to confession. He had little time to eat, rest, or have a personal life. He died, exhausted, from helping people, often 18 hours a day.

I wanted to be like him and asked the two priests, Newton and Hogan, how I could do this. By that fall they had made arrangements for me to enter the Holy Cross religious community and be in the seminary at Notre Dame University, operated by the Holy Cross Fathers. I did not have any fears or doubts about going and went off to South Bend that fall. My parents drove me across the flatlands of Ohio and Indiana.

My health had recovered and I felt ready for this. I was excited. I had also developed a strong desire to study about the existence of God. I wanted to find evidence in books that God existed, and how the world came to be. I was really talking about theology and philosophy, but did not know it.

Prayer

"Leaving home was a big event in life. I was 19. Lord, you were 30. The university world brought me more into the learning process, and then came the call of near-death. This led to a lifelong fascination with death and what might follow.

"You were getting a grip on me, but I hardly knew it."

main campus, looking toward the university and the golden dome and the cavelike candle-filled grotto of the shrine to Mary.

I learned to read in Latin, went to the exciting football games of an undefeated team, savored walks and talks around the lake, and enjoyed the times of silence. Most of all, I loved the Gregorian chants of the liturgy, especially on Sundays when we joined the hundred or so older seminarians from the "Major Sem" across another lake, in the main church on campus.

This wonderful American Gothic church structure, with its giant altar for the liturgy, choir stalls for our singing, and so many architectural pleasures, was my favorite place on campus. It had a second golden altar under a dome dedicated to Mary, sent to the university from France by a relative of Napoleon. Light filtered through a skylight above. The organ was wonderful too, and the bell had a great solemn toll. I loved to go in procession down the long aisles, in black robes covered by white surplices, singing; it seemed what heaven would be. I was 20 years old.

This church has been modernized today, but is still beautiful with some good new additions, including the statue of the dead Christ in the arms of Mary by the famous refugee Yugoslavian sculptor, Ivan Mestrovic. He lived at Notre Dame while I was there and left his mark everywhere with monumental sculptures. He fled Communism in his country, and the university built him a small studio where he could work. Rumor had it he used nude models. All of his sculptures, now scattered around the university, are powerful, spiritual. We never miss looking for them when we visit Notre Dame.

In the Latin class I met a man named John Dierna who later became a probation officer in Elyria, worked with me when I was a young social worker, and became a lifelong friend. He is retired now as a federal parole officer and works in downtown Elyria in the Municipal Court. He was a "character witness" at my trial.

At the close of that year there was a vacation at home for awhile, and then I left for the novitiate at South Bend, the next step in entering a religious community. One becomes a "novice," that is a newcomer to a way of life, a learner of new ways. In this case, the ways of the Holy Cross Fathers community, and the ways of religious communal life. This would lead to taking vows of poverty, chastity, and obedience, the traditional promises of such communities.

There were 24 of us entering the novitiate that year, living together in the former home of the Studebaker family, a mansion in South Bend given to the university for such use.

It was an immense wooden Tudor house with many rooms, including a chapel, dining room for all of us, recreation room in the basement, swimming pool outside, nice gardens and grounds, and a carriage house for classes. All the rooms and walls in the big house were paneled in soft, rich dark brown wood. The floors were wood also.

One priest was in charge of each group of novices for the year, and he was called the Novice Master, sounding kind of formal. Ours was an ascetic, tall, thin man with a good sense of humor. He was kindly and interested that each of us would turn out to be good members of his community, if we took that step at the end of the year.

Taken at the Holy Cross novitiate in South Bend. That's my Aunt Mary Wimmers on the left, who lived with us for many years, dying at the age of ninety-three.

A lot happened to me that year spiritually. We spent all of the day in silence, except for 15 minutes or so after dinner and on special religious feast days, like Christmas and Easter, when we might talk all afternoon.

We did not see newspapers or TV so the world's distractions were not on us. It is so easy not to know about the latest plane crash, Wall Street problems, presidential sneeze.

We had assigned duties, like cleaning the hall, the chapel, and other areas. I was in charge of the small greenhouse, raising flowers mostly for the chapel. Sometimes we worked outside on the grounds. The few times we went swimming or played outside, it was in silence. Sometimes we cheated on the talking and whispered bits of news about someone leaving or the content of the coming meal. In such an atmosphere, small things become big things. We would laugh uncontrollably at meals when we ate celery. Twenty-five silent people munching on celery makes a funny sound.

I learned patience, the value of silence, the importance of taking time to reflect before jumping into things.

We did have classes and a few professors spoke to us. Classes on the history and spirit of the Holy Cross Community, on the spiritual life, on praying, and on the liturgy, which is the public worship, the official services of the Catholic church.

This was the most important class of the week for me, taught by Holy Cross Father Michael Mathis, a small man who jumped up and down when he described how exciting the Mass and other services should be, even funerals, weddings, singing psalms and the Liturgy of the Hours. I picked up his enthusiasm and we remained friends for years. The University of Notre Dame Center for Pastoral Liturgy now has an annual award in honor of Michael Mathis. In 1989 it was given to the International Commissions on English in the Liturgy.

As part of our prayer life, we chanted the Office of the Blessed Virgin Mary in the morning and during the day. This is a shorter version of the official daily church liturgy sung by monks. In this version the psalms and prayers mostly honor Mary, the Mother of Christ.

We sang the different hours in a simple Gregorian chant, with some melodies for hymns. I came to love the slow, mystical, almost hypnotic sound of the chant as it was done from early morning to bedtime, seven different times during the day.

I became intensely involved in the life of a novice, praying long hours in the chapel, sometimes alone, reading books about God and holy people who had lived in other times, the saints. I was now 21 years old and it was 1950.

In my youthful enthusiasm I wrote up a secret dedication of myself to Christ and it went like this: "You already know that I belong entirely to you. I tell you so often. Yet I am so weak and of myself am in such great danger of losing you that at this midnight Mass of 1950 I am going to consecrate every bit of myself to your infant Sacred Heart forever and ever. This means a full giving of myself for your use. I will no longer exist for my own pleasure and use.

"I am yours wholly and entirely to be used in any way you wish. I will have no cares that are not yours. I am as nothing, completely yours. Come and fill me. Use me for the glory of your father and to console your heart by making me love you daily more and more and permitting me to save many souls. I trust completely in you and abandon myself to the mercy and love of your Sacred Heart. I am yours. Attach me to you alone.

"I call upon all of your heaveny saints to see that I fulfill my offering in this consecration. In particular I call upon the Cure'of Ars (St John Vianney) and your Little Flower (St Therese) to keep me faithful. Daily they will tell me how your Sacred Heart desires me to act. The Cure' will be my particular messenger between your heart and the world. He will help me with many of my problems so you will be free to work in me.

"Finally, since I am consecrating myself to your Infant Heart I will become very little like you so that your mother may come and carry me to you when you are ready for my soul. I am hers for your heart. Mary, help me to remain near his heart. Jesus, hold me tightly until I am with you."

* * * * * * * * *

The life of a novice turned out like the year in Dayton. I grew exhausted with the intensity. After 10 months we all

THOU SHALT BE WIH ME
IN PARADISE

Luke XXIII, 43.

T. Peters

The front and back of the card with the 1950 prayer I wrote in the novitiate. I still use this to mark the opening of the Liturgy of the Hours each day.

decided I should return home to rest before I had another lung collapse. My chest seemed in pain.

It was very difficult but one day I packed my few personal things, turned in the clothes of a novice, the black robe, hat, belt, and said goodbye to friends of these two years, and left for home.

Monsignor Newton put me to work in the parish house again, I also worked for a neighbor farmer next to my New Havoc home, and in a few months felt better.

I decided to try the seminary again.

Prayer

"Priests continued to influence my life. Monsignor Newton and Father Hogan are gone from my world now. I look forward to seeing them again. With St. John Vianney they were instrumental in leading me to the seminary where I met you, O Jesus, and the Father, Son and Holy Spirit, and learned the value of silence and meditation and prayer.

"Looking back, I now know how much those years were important in helping me live out the rest of my life."

Chapter 10

St. Charles Seminary, Summers in Appalachia, Father Connors

With the advice of Msgr. Newton I decided to study as a diocesan seminarian and applied in Columbus, Ohio. The Cleveland diocese felt I might get exhausted again. Cleveland had lots of priestly applicants at the time, and Columbus, being a "Baptist Belt" area, had few. A diocesan seminary trains priests for parishes rather than for religious communities, like the Holy Cross Fathers where I had been. My intention was to become a parish priest in the diocese of Columbus, which would mean completing my two years of college and taking four years more of Theology.

Columbus had its own college seminary, St. Charles Borromeo, but sent people to a school called Mount St. Mary's of the West in Cincinnati for the four years of Theology. I entered St. Charles as a college junior. This is a very small school in one building on East Broad Street, near Bexley, a wealthy suburb of Columbus. There were a dozen of us in a class, taking Philosophy, English, History, etc., leading to a Bachelor of Arts Degree. An English professor, my best priest friend there, taught us to read a book a day, skim reading, and to read slower for pleasure. My Philosophy professor, Paul "Doc"

Glenn, weighed about 300 pounds, taught with his eyes shut, using one of the many books he had written in Latin. Sometime he talked in Latin, but easy Latin we could understand rather than the classical of Cicero.

It seemed Doc Glenn always had his eyes shut except when we were not paying attention or when someone wanted to sneak out of the room. Then his immense head would turn up and eyes would open wide to focus on the poor student, who shriveled to nothing. He would then be questioned on the matter Glenn was discussing.

I had never studied philosophy before and began to learn how to use reason to think through the questions of experience, matter, logic, government, the things of our human existence. Understanding them without any theology or scripture. Reasoning—it was fascinating, especially in the preciseness of Latin.

A couple of new spiritual insights stand out from those two years in Columbus. First, I was in the cathedral choir, as were all seminarians, in downtown Columbus, and second, I came to know the cloistered convent of Carmelite nuns a block from the seminary. And two other different kinds of life experiences happened in the next two summer vacations. I met the rural Appalachian people of Ohio and I met delinquents in an institution. These experiences also became lasting ones.

The cathedral choir traveled the several miles to downtown Columbus to the cream colored, sandstone Gothic cathedral of our bishop to help perform all the major ceremonies of the feasts of the year and the main Mass each Sunday.

In those days, ceremonies with bishops had more pomp, music, ritual, mystery, and color than now, and were in Latin. We went in solemn procession in our robes down the long aisle, passing between pews filled with people, and entered the choir stalls on either side of the altar. Here we sang our intricate Gregorian chants, different for each service, and our hymn melodies, sometimes in complicated polyphonic music, beyond doing with my partially tone deaf capabilities.

During these two years I was really enjoying the feasts and seasons of the liturgical year, with the changing moods of the

Graduation from college at St. Charles, in Columbus, Ohio. I'm 2nd from the right, row 2. Most of my classmates went on to become priests, but I only saw one of them once in the years after. That's "Doc" Paul Glenn in the center, our philosophy prof and author of many books, in many languages.

ceremonies and music; Holy Week and Easter were my favorite times. We banged our heavy hymn books on our choir stalls in the darkness of the church singing Tenebrae, a sad ceremony marking the death of Christ. The loud slamming of books was to signify the world of purgatory, a frightening place, where Christ was perhaps abandoned after his death and before the resurrection.

I also liked to go to the Carmelite convent, which was in a beautiful old mansion donated to the nuns by a rich person in Bexley. The convent was a block from the seminary. The Carmelites are a hundreds of years old community, named for a place of prayer in the Old Testament, Mount Carmel. Their house was similar to my novitiate in South Bend, but smaller.

Here about 20 nuns lived in seclusion. Two nuns, called externs, because they worked outside the cloister, answered the door and talked with people, serving cookies and milk to most guests.

There was a small dark paneled chapel open to visitors, and a wooden grate along one wall, with a burlap curtain the other side of the grate, hiding the nuns' chapel. During the day the nuns would chant the liturgy, the "hours," in their high-pitched, delicate Gregorian melodies, seeming like angels to me. In the darkened chapel, a few candles burning, the music would come through and give me goose bumps. It was heavenlike.

I volunteered to serve Mass there at 6:30 many mornings and would walk over with a priest from the seminary, sometimes talking quietly, sometimes in silence.

When one of the nuns died I was there to serve the funeral Mass. We went inside the wall, into the cloister, where this calm, beautiful woman rested in a plain wooden coffin in her brown robes. So simple, passing from this life to the next as if it were almost one and the same for her.

Later, as a social worker, I would bring my Lorain, Ohio, street gangs to Columbus to see the state penetentiary, the electric chair, the capital, and this convent. They would sit quietly in the chapel and hear the nuns singing in the otherwise silence, eat some cookies, and share this mystery. They always said it was the high point of their trip. They knew what the other places might be like, but this was so different from their street lives.

This Carmelite convent is no longer cloistered. Now the nuns work with people in the city, teaching spirituality, a more active vocation.

At home on a holiday I had another life-lasting experience.

Father Hogan asked me to serve Mass for him on Christmas at the county home for the aged, a place called Golden Acres, outside Elyria. We arrived at 6:30 a.m. and went to a small room with a table for an altar and about 25 people in attendance, some in wheelchairs, and a stern, large woman they called "the matron" looking on. This Mass was a blur for me, too much to take in.

After the liturgy we made the rounds to say hello to the bedridden. This took me into three buildings of people, sad looking people, some just getting up. There were few signs of Christmas anywhere.

We had to pass through one small room to get to another larger room and in this small room was a man on a bed, fully-clothed, tossing back and forth, groaning, covered with an old blanket. The matron matter-of-factly said he was dying.

On the way back through the same room we stopped and Father Hogan talked with him a long time, until the man calmed down and seemed to be at peace. I could not hear the conversation, but I gathered the man did not much believe in God. After the talk with Father Hogan he had some kind of faith and was ready to die.

We went on to other areas, but the sight of that man stayed with me. Dying, all alone, in a pass-through room. Later in my life this memory stirred me to want to work with people who were dying alone.

In the summers I had to spend my months working in the Columbus diocese, assisting a priest. The first summer I was sent to Millersburg, Ohio, an Amish area, teaching summer bible schools in these Appalachian hills. I visited the people of Killbuck, people on back mountain roads, people I came to love for their lifestyle and open ways. One family got me drunk on their moonshine. They thought it was hilarious.

I have always had an association with Appalachian causes

since then, belonging to the Council of the Southern Mountains for years, and still visiting Berea College in Berea, Ky., the center of Appalachian studies.

The second summer was in Sugar Grove, Ohio, outside Lancaster. A small, rural parish. The priest, Father William Connors, was also chaplain of the nearby Boys Industrial School, a state institution for over a thousand boys, delinquents. I went there every Sunday with Father Connors and got to know this world which was all new to me and became such a big part of my life.

Father Connors moved on to other juvenile institutions, next a chaplain in prisons, ending up at Ohio's biggest, Lucasville, where the new electric chair sits. Our friendship continued over the years and I spent a day with him in Lucasville before he retired. It was this day that led to the Monasteries idea, put together years later in leave of absence from Betterway during the long time of my trial.

After that summer I entered The Major Seminary in Cincinnati. This included two more summers of study back at Notre Dame University in South Bend.

Prayer

"O Lord you continued to lead me still more into the world of learning and prayer through the Carmelites, the cathedral ceremonies of liturgy, classes in philosophy and Latin. I loved all this more than I knew.

"Then you introduced me to the worlds of Appalachia and delinquent boys. Two areas that would be a big part of my life, social work with poor and troubled people, yet people with so much good in them.

"Thank you for beginning to awaken in me feelings for the sufferings of others."

Chapter 11

St. Mary's Seminary, Notre Dame University, and Chicago

After the summer in Sugar Grove I moved for schooling into a big building atop a hill in Norwood, a suburb of Cincinnati, overlooking the Procter and Gamble plant, the home of Ivory soap. Once a week when they cleaned some vats the air smelled like a heavy dose of soap. It burned our eyes and nostrils.

Mount St. Mary's was an imposing, columned, stone structure, like a Greek temple. The Archbishop of Cincinnati lived next door in a smaller version of the same.

Almost 300 men from all over the country studied theology here. They did the final four years of priesthood training for many diocesan bishops who did not have their own seminary.

We studied Sacred Scripture, many aspects of theology, homiletics (preaching) and related subjects. There was lots of homework and we lived two in a room, with hours of study in silence every night. It was hard work. We took walks in our black robes around the small seminary grounds. We were old enough to vote, and we were counted as residents of the area, which meant we could change some elections because there were so many of us. We also counted in the percentage of young men in the district to be drafted, but we were exempt. It was years later I learned that some neighborhood people did not like us for these reasons. Their sons got drafted. We did not.

During those two years I made friends with lots of men, and some are priests and bishops now. Others left before ordination, as I did.

The chapel there was large, bright with gold, a rounded ceiling; we all faced the center aisle from the left and right side of the church. The liturgy was solemn, but not like in the cathedral in Columbus, because the chapel was not as impressive in style. I did not go to the Cincinnati cathedral to sing because my voice was not good enough. The cathedral there is big and starkly simple, white in color, designed by Christopher Wren, the Englishman who designed William and Mary College in Williamsburg and many American churches.

The most important things that happened to me spiritually those two years took place away from the seminary, although I did learn a lot in theology and scripture classes.

I spent the two summers at the University of Notre Dame, sent there to get a master's degree in sacred liturgy. I was the seminary barber in Cincinnati so I put up a sign at Notre Dame, charging 50 cents a head in my room to get extra spending money.

It was wonderful to be back at Notre Dame, and I did not know until then how much I liked the place. I went over to the "Little Sem" to find people I knew and saw a few. But mostly in those two summers I got to know interesting people from all over this country and the world. The university brought famous scholars and "doers" to South Bend for the summers to teach and share their ideas. Some became my haircut customers. Msgr. Davis was a scripture scholar from England, Msgr. Martin Hellriegel was performing liturgy in English in St. Louis, building bonfires in church for Easter, and exciting the people of his parish with a new spirit of liturgy.

A Benedictine monk from Belgium, Dom Vitry, taught us his special brand of Gregorian chant, flowing up and down the scale. He brought in women from Grailville, outside Cincinnati to dance to the psalms in the liturgy. A priest in Canada,

Father Gelineau, was writing melodies to English psalms to sound like the ancient Hebrew music and asked Dom Vitry to teach his psalms to us to see how they sounded. These became the famous Gelineau Psalms. We also experimented with the Mass in English, although this was not officially approved by the church yet. I studied church architecture with a Benedictine monk who helped design the modern monastic church at Collegeville, Minn.

Father Johannes Hofinger was there from a seminary in the Philippines. For years he had been teaching in China but had to leave because of the revolution. He spoke German, French, Chinese, and some other languages, but not English. The day before he was to start teaching class we met in a cafeteria and he asked me to help him with his English for his class in Kerygmatic Catechetics. This was an approach based on love of God rather than fear of God, and leading to the elimination of the old fear-filled Baltimore Catechism. That course became his first book in English, and we became good friends. He stayed at New Havoc a week on one of his cross country trips. This new approach viewed God as a loving father, to be obeyed out of love, rather than the fear of hell.

Msgr. Reynold Hillenbrand was there from Chicago, and we talked day after day. He made me come to Chicago to learn about his Young Christian Students groups, the Young Christian Workers, and the Christian Family Movement. He brought this small group idea over from Europe where it successfully combatted Communist cell groups. The founder of the Young Christian Workers was Canon Joseph Cardijn.

For years Hillenbrand was head of the seminary in Chicago and taught his priests the importance and role of the laity, the liturgy, and so many new things. I met with some of his cell groups in Chicago and heard young laypeople talking about how they loved Christ and wanted to spread this to their friends in school and at work. It was amazing to me to hear young people my age, not in the seminary, talking about Christ so openly.

They told me to go find Friendship House and Peter Maurin House and I did, and these experiences profoundly influenced me.

Friendship House was an idea of a former aristocratic Russian baroness, Catherine DeHueck, whose wealthy husband died when they came to this country during their revolution. She volunteered to help in the poor sections of a big city. One thing led to another and soon she was opening storefronts in black neighborhoods and housing projects. The places were called Friendship House and gave out clothing and food, like the hospitality centers of today. I got to know a Friendship House program in the middle of the crowded, all black, South Side of Chicago.

Catherine eventually married a newspaper writer, Eddie Doherty, and they moved to Combermere, Ontario, Canada, and founded an international organization of lay people and priests called Madonna House. Mary and I visited there in 1987, just before Catherine died. Eddie became a priest in the Eastern Rite Catholic Church and had died earlier.

I kept up with Baroness Catherine and her work and introduced her when she gave a talk in Cleveland a few years after my Chicago experience.

Peter Maurin House in Chicago was part of the Catholic Worker Movement, a loosely organized string of houses in big cities offering free meals and places to stay to the homeless. It was started by Dorothy Day and Peter Maurin in 1930. In 1989 it included about 100 houses, hotels, and farms going by the name Catholic Worker.

Peter Maurin was a thinker and talker who felt people should live off the land and live simply, not wasting the goods of this earth. Dorothy Day, his friend, had been a young Communist worker in New York City and became a Catholic and opened houses for the poor as an alternative to Communism. The name Catholic Worker was part of that alternative, and they published a penny paper by the same name, which is still printed monthly. It is mailed to 90,000 people across the country, and is still a penny. Later in life I got some of the ideas for our Betterway newspaper from this paper.

I visited Maryhouse, a Catholic Worker home for women off the Bowery, shortly before Dorothy died. I never talked to her but did read all her writings and sent some Elyria people to her places in New York City. I saw Dorothy when she preached at the funeral of Bill Gauchat at Our Lady of the Wayside in Avon Lake, near Elyria. She was saintly looking, spoke of Bill's goodness, was almost angelic in her old age.

Back to those days in Chicago: I took a bus one day to Peter Maurin House, in the middle of a slum just on the downtown Chicago fringes. The volunteers there put me on a truck to take a load of sandwiches and vats of soup over to nearby Madison Street to feed the men of Skid Row.

We parked the truck at a glass strewn block-wide vacant lot. Hundreds of men were sitting and laying around. I was scared. My first job was to hand a bowl of soup to each of the 700 men we fed each night, at dusk. Slowly I got comfortable with the men, and began to talk with individuals. They told me their stories: broken homes, lost brothers and sisters, terrible drinking problems, leaving their home towns, coming to Chicago and other skid row areas. There were 10,000 men here and 7,000 women. They no longer bothered me with their smell, dirty clothes, swollen purple faces, missing legs, cuts, dirty bandages. These disappeared as they became Eddie, Bill, Sam, Phil. I never met the women because they did not come to the big yard, but I saw them on the streets and curbs countless times.

One small Skid Row scene changed some parts of my life: I was riding on a bus one Saturday to Peter Maurin House and a thin old Black man had fallen in the streets. He looked very drunk and was trying to get up. Three white people in black clothes, a man and two women, were leaning over him like vultures, bibles in hand, shouting, and waving. I could hear them, but did not understand what they were saying.

This split-second sight of the perversion of religion burned in my mind. Why were they preaching at him and not helping him up? How can people get religion when they are down and out? Religion must work for social justice, must help the needy, or it is hollow and empty. Tinkling brass. I wanted to help that old black man. I still see him.

Carl Merschel, an artist volunteer at Peter Maurin House sold me a Rouault engraving later that year. It shows, in black and white, a French worker at his bench, looking down and beat, worn out. It is titled: "John Francis does not sing Alleluia."

John Francis cannot enjoy the beautiful liturgy of the church, the chants I had come to love, because he is too tired. He is treated too badly by his world of work.

This picture hangs beside me as I type this book.

The studies ended at Notre Dame one summer before I got that master's degree, but the learning stayed. My whole view of the approach to teaching religion changed, to the Kerygmatic, love based. We try to please God because we love God. The "do not do that and do not do this" teaching was gone. I learned to love the liturgy in English. I walked the campus of Notre Dame at night, savoring the mystical feeling of the statue of Mary above the university, the golden dome.

I remember one night when Cardinal Cody came from Chicago for a big celebration honoring Mary. Thousands of nuns, priests and lay people walked around the two lakes, carrying candles which reflected off the waters that dark night, walking in a great procession, seemingly endless. Walking toward the grotto shrine, itself lit with hundreds of candles. The Cardinal led the rosary and we led hymns. It seemed like one of the foretastes of heaven that have come into my life.

That summer Father Hofinger and I would often walk over to St. Mary's College to talk with Mother Mary Madeleva, the president of the school, and a widely known poet. She would read poems to us, and talk about China with him. She seemed so ordinary, not like the president of a college or a poet. She was thin, gentle, precise. She gave me an early Christmas gift, a book of her collected poems, and wrote inside: "for you, in the beautiful spirit of Christmas tide. Sister M. Madeleva."

I met Jean Charlot, a French-Hawaiian-Mexican artist who did most of his art work in frescoes, color mixed into cement and applied to walls to make pictures and designs. He had me helping him at Notre Dame and St. Mary's, where his frescoes still decorate the outside of some of the buildings, big bold pictures. He drew me as a skinny flat-topped seminarian in one of the books and gave me his painting of a dark skinned peasant woman and child, Mexican appearing.

Those summers at Notre Dame brought me into the modern church, whether I was to be a priest or a lay person. They also helped me find Christ in quiet places, the little side chapels in the big church, the grotto, the chapels in every building on the campus, the two lakes, the golden dome.

I never miss an opportunity to stop at Notre Dame and walk around the campus and the lakes, savoring the past.

Prayer

"Dear Lord, you continued to enrich my life with theology as I learned more about you and experienced the new liturgy in my church, sung in English, spoken in English. You also led me into the life of Chicago and the skid row of that fascinating city. Here I discovered your face in men and women of the streets, with their terrible alcohol problems. And I loved those people."

The Catholic Worker newspaper masthead, by Ade Bethune.

Chapter 12

Seminary Days End; Farming, Social Work

These two summers at Notre Dame and in Chicago were very rich for me. In Chicago I met social activists, like Ed Marciniak, who for years fought city hall. He did it so well Mayor Richard Daley finally hired him to correct some of the racial and economic injustices in that city from within. Marciniak is still doing that in the 90's, an elder radical statesman in the Windy City.

I met the editor of a Catholic union paper and became friends with him and his wife. He was white, she black, and they had to live in the black south side because of housing patterns. He gave me his address and I visited one Sunday, surprised to get off the "El" train in an all black neighborhood. They moved to Europe where he had another newspaper, last I knew.

I have returned to Chicago many times, to the Greek restaurants on Halsted, and to the "thieves market" on Sundays further down Halsted on Maxwell Street, listening to street corner jazz and blues on every block. Blacks and Jews competed for business, love and health potions were sold by turbaned men and women, and pickpockets were active.

My spiritual experiences in Chicago came from Skid Row, and I still go there when I can.

All of these Chicago adventures took me into the world of black people and poor people, and I remain there today in my heart.

At the end of the summers I would return to Cincinnati.

At St. Mary's seminary I became friends with Clarence Rivers, later a priest, a black priest, who became widely known for writing African sounding music for Catholic liturgy, using the name Clancy Rivers. He is still experimenting with his music, and many of his songs are national favorites, including "Ride On King Jesus," a spirited Palm Sunday song.

Clancy opened up another area in my life, the role of women in the church and in the world. He told me about a place nearby called Grailville, in Loveland, Ohio, just outside Cinci. He was going there to sing his music and said I should get to know the women who lived there.

One weekend I went over. I found almost a hundred women together living like a commune, raising food by working the soil by hand labor. They also had some cows and were "living off the land." They wore peasant clothing. They had worship and liturgy that was just to my taste, singing psalms, chanting.

I found out they were part of a worldwide group of laywomen in the Catholic church teaching in many countries, holding workshops on the role of women in the world, before this was a popular subject. They were headquartered in Grailville, had a book and gift shop, and produced some of their own art. The art was strong and contemporary.

There were many more visits. The women converted a large barn into a church painted white inside and out that was outstanding in its simplicity. I met Trina Paulus, from Cleveland, an artist and writer. When we opened the Search Shop her mother brought a lot of Trina's work to us and helped set up the store. At that time Trina was in Israel teaching tapestry. Some of her art is now produced in quantity and sold by Abbey Press.

From those days at Grailville I developed a special interest in women's roles. I went to see the art show of Judy Chicago. We carry a lot of women related books and cards at the Search Shop. Years late I was thrilled when I saw and heard the first woman Anglican priest dressed in full vestments at our parish in Elyria.

One of the women who worked at Betterway, Sister Marietta Starrie, C.S.J., was very involved in feminist ideas. She works a lot to get prayer language to fit men and women instead of men only.

At the end of my second year of theology I left the seminary for the last time. I had two more years of theology to complete before ordination to the priesthood. It was again a difficult time for me, and to clear my head I went to work back on the farm next to my parent, picking tomatoes and hauling vegetables to the Farmers Market in Cleveland. Even though it was a down time in my spirits, I recovered in a summer. During those six seminary years I did learn a lot about the existence of God and about the world we live in. I knew that God existed from reasoning and my religion. To arrive at this point was one of the reasons I entered the seminary.

By now I spoke good Spanish and Msgr. Newton told me that the local Catholic Charities needed a Spanish speaking social worker in Lorain to help the newly arrived Puerto Rican families, imported to work in the steel mill there.

I had no idea what social work was, but they hired me, and I started my career. I got to know the pastor of the Lorain Spanish chapel, Father Gerard Frederick, who later became head of his religious community, the Trinitarians. They work with the poor of the world, Hispanic, Indians, and Blacks.

He taught me his brand of social work, which was to pull strings and solve problems for his people. He coped with welfare problems, job problems, family quarrels, drinking, fighting, street kids who could not speak English and would not go to school.

His church was a small converted meat market off Vine Avenue in South Lorain, near the steel mill street with its permanent haze of red dust in the air. Years later I proposed marriage to Mary in this tiny chapel before a large painting of Our Lady of Guadalupe.

I thought a social worker should be sociable, like the name said. So I found the poorest section of Lorain, an area outside the city called Campito, "the little field," and began to walk the mud streets, getting to know the people living in homemade houses, shacks, chicken coops, tents, lean-to buildings. Puerto Rican people, Appalachians, even Mexican migrants who left this area where they lived to work the beet fields of Western Ohio and Michigan. Lots of alcoholics, the mix of poor and the problems of the poor.

They were almost the same as the people of skid row in Chicago, but not adrift yet from their communities. Some of the kids would be someday.

I visited every house, drank "cafe con leche," a strong coffee with hot sweetened milk, ate rice and beans, and learned Spanish as it is spoken in the hills of Puerto Rico, rather than the castles of Spain as I had been taught.

One of my remedies for family problems was to place the kids in a Catholic Charities facility, Parmadale, the place run by the Sisters of Charity, whom I knew years earlier. This was a beautiful setting in Parma, Ohio, a suburb of Cleveland, designed for the orphan children of European immigrants. But there were no more orphans. With the help of Social Security, kids now lived with relatives when the parents died.

Parmadale was down in numbers of kids when I suggested they take the poor kids of Lorain. They had never had black or Hispanic boys or girls there before and this was strange for the nuns. I took the kids there anyhow and tried to tell them the nuns would like them. Because these were the same nuns who owned Forest View Farm, of my childhood, I had an "in" with them and they accepted my placements even if they didn't fully approve. I even got them to hire a layman to run one of the unit "cottages." Ten years later this man, John Bazley, left there and helped start Betterway. He was the first lay person to run a "cottage" at Parmadale and had been a childhood friend of mine.

During these years I liked going to Mass in the Spanish chapel in Lorain because the people were joyful and spontaneous and lively. I also started going to Lorain's St. Nicholas church, a Byzantine parish where the singing was in English and Greek. Roman Catholic churches still used Latin, which I understood, but I was for the use of the vernacular because of my experiences at Notre Dame. I saw how beautiful and meaningful English could be. I came to love the Byzantine music and ceremonies.

My days in Lorain as a social worker were exciting and I began to learn about the local politics, the gambling that took so much family money, the prostitution, the workings of a steel town. I wanted to change some things but people told me I did not have the training, since I did not have a master's degree in social work.

After hearing this too often I decided to get a master's degree. Catholic Charities said they would pay part of the tuition and living costs if I would work for them for two years after the schooling.

I looked for a place to study and chose Boston College, mostly to see the ocean and the East coast, having never been there.

They accepted me into the Graduate School of Social Work and I looked forward to two years in Boston and schooling with the Jesuits, my first experience with them.

Prayer

"My formal days of learning about religion came to an end after six years. Those times have influenced all the rest of my life more than I ever thought they would. I am eternally grateful.

"Then, through the suggestion of Monsignor Newton, and the bent I had from those Chicago adventures, I entered social work, where I would remain from then on. Lord, your love for me is so wonder-filled. Lead me and guide me forever."

Chapter 13

Boston College, Harvard, Cape Cod

I made the 17-hour trip to Boston in my VW Beetle, and went back and forth that way for holidays the next two years. Usually I had two or three passengers from the Cleveland area who were also in school there.

Arrangements were made by mail for me to rent a room on Beacon Street, at the bottom of Beacon Hill, next to the Boston Garden and Common, and as it turned out, a block from a bar named The Bull and Finch Pub (Cheers).

Boston and the address sounded exciting and it was, except I arrived in the dark in the rain and was told it was not safe to leave anything in the car overnight. My VW was packed with a lot of books, and my room was a fifth floor walk-up, a long haul. I carried books up the stairs for hours.

A dozen students and government workers shared rooms in this narrow brick house, 150 years old. We shared the baths and later the kitchen and food, as we got to know one another. The bigger downstairs apartments had their own kitchens and bath and were occupied year round by older working people. Across the street was a very proper finishing school for proper girls. I did not believe such things existed anymore. The Kathryn Gibbs School taught manners to wealthy, socialite girls, who lived there for a period of time to become proper Bostonians.

I fell in love with Boston and still return every few years to walk the streets of Beacon Hill and stroll the Garden and Common, where flowers mix with humanity to make a show, along with the graceful swan boats.

Boston is not big and rough like Chicago. With 27 universities and colleges in the area, it was a student's world, along with the government workers in the buildings two blocks from me. Harvard and M.I.T. were only 10 minutes away and Harvard became my second home, wandering hours in the book stores and museums and around the campus.

My favorite church in the Boston area was at Harvard, St. Paul's. The choir director knew all about the liturgy and how to make it beautiful, directing the large congregation, mostly Harvard students and faculty, and staging wonderful long processions around the inside of the church to add grandeur and dignity to the ceremonies. I also liked to go to Mass in the very small chapel at M.I.T. It was round, brick, and sat on a moat of water so that the water reflected from the base onto the inside and outside walls, creating a shimmering rippling light on their surfaces all the time. It was almost distracting, but did seem other-worldly.

There were two churches in downtown Boston near me, the Paulist Fathers chapel on the Boston Common on Park Street, and a large modernistic, garish, place run by Franciscans. Masses were every half hour at the Franciscan place, seemingly day and night, and there was no sense of liturgy or community, just someone saying a fast Mass so people could go. The liturgy was ordinary at the much smaller Paulist chapel, but the sermons were excellent, the best in Boston. I found out the Paulists were known for their preaching.

My classes in graduate school were near my room, on Newbury Street, a very chic fashionable avenue of art shops, fancy clothes, Bonwit Teller, F.A.O. Schwartz for toys, and the like. There were little restaurants and sidewalk cafes and it was all very cosmopolitan, similar to what I later found in Paris, Amsterdam, other world cities.

I learned to stop with the other students in the bars like

Cheers and have a drink in the late afternoon and eat a meal of free snacks. When they would see that it was only one drink and lots of cheese, shrimp, crackers, bacon, etc. they would give us bad looks and we would go somewhere else, to return weeks later when the manager forgot, or was new.

Days and nights I walked the streets of Beacon Hill, which is topped off by the domed state capital designed by Christopher Wren. These are cobblestone streets, room for one-way traffic, with a line of parked cars on one side. There are no front yards and the houses touch one another, their wooden doors with brass knockers right along the sidewalk. It seemed like something out of Dickens. Charles Street, at the foot of Beacon Hill, was the local neighborhood shopping area with small grocery stores with fruits and vegetables displayed outside in bins. Sidewalks in front of florist shops were filled with colorful flowers and plants. There were a dozen or more antique shops, several restaurants, the Charles St. VW Garage, and at least one church, Unitarian I believe.

During these two years of school we had to do real social work under close supervision. My first year was at the V.A. hospital in Rutland, outside Worcester. I lived at the hospital three days a week, working with tubercular alcoholic people, mostly men, many dying. Some had lived on skid row and told me the details of their lives. I had to prepare some to die, others to get government benefits, or reconcile with their families. Alcohol was plentiful in most rooms, smuggled in by employees and relatives, bought with the government funds everyone received. I wore a white gown and mask and all the nurses called me "doctor." Memories of my own year of T.B. were plentiful and I developed a sympathetic cough with the patients.

The second year I did family counseling in the Boston Family Service Association on Beacon Hill, counseling kids and families. The agency was on Joy Street, a few blocks from my home.

Weekends and vacations some of us in school headed for the ocean, taking a cabin on Cape Cod, which began a love affair in my life with the Cape. The rolling, sometimes roaring, endless waves of surf captivate and relax me. I can walk the beach for hours. As students we had a cabin in the town of Orleans, halfway to the end of the Cape, and I still go there with Mary. The ocean is also a place where I like to read psalms, with their many references to water.

I spent a weekend alone at the tip of the Cape in Provincetown in the winter. I came to like the Portuguese fishermen who are also alone in the winter, with the tourists and residents moving south.

In Orleans I found the church of St. Joan of Arc, and Mary and I still go there, only now they have a big new church building, all white and clean, a little like Grailville. Back then it was a very small wooden cabin-like structure which is now abandoned.

During the two years at Boston College I learned a lot about psychology and medicine and interviewing. I did come to see God in the many faces of the peoples of the world living in Boston, so different from people I knew, and in the faces of those who slept and drank in the Boston Common. I also met some authentic Boston Irish, who bought a bucket of baked beans for dinner every Saturday.

One day in the Boston Common I heard a fiery talk by a newcomer to the national scene, Martin Luther King. Another time I went to a parade honoring a folk hero from Cuba, Fidel Castro. He rode in an open convertible and wore those familiar army fatigues. Everyone cheered Castro; a small crowd cheered King.

Toward the end of my two years in Boston I began to get an irritation in my left eye. I went around the corner from my house to the Boston Eye Hospital, a big place specializing in eye surgery.

After weeks of testing the chief surgeon told me I had an unusual case of glaucoma, and also unusual in that I was not yet 30. He would have to operate. When school ended he did that and once again health problems threw me into the care of God, making me pray that I would be able to see all right. At first I was "blind" because my eyes were both covered for some days after the operation in the hospital, but after that I could see. I spent a month with friends at the ocean to be near the hospital and the doctor.

There was yet another people experience in Boston. I got to know a family living in Columbia Point, a famous housing project which was a world in itself. It was just south of downtown Boston, and was later torn down for the location of the John F. Kennedy Library and Museum. It was terrible. People were robbed and killed in the elevators, behind buildings, in their homes. It was totally unsafe. A priest and nun ran a small center in one building, but no other social services existed. It was so dangerous and was isolated from everything, no stores, no hospital. The only solution was to eventually tear it down.

I learned something from that about government bureaucratic planning for poor people, how awful it can be and how it can bring out the worst in anyone. I walked around and went to see my friends and felt the isolation and terror of life there. How could a highly paid, educated group of people plan and build such a terrible place where none of them would ever live?

Hell on earth, it was called by my friends.

Prayer

"O Jesus, how much I loved Boston, Harvard, and the waves and roar of the ocean. You allowed me to continually find the beauties of our world.

"Sitting and watching the tides come and go became a great image of eternity in my mind. How marvelous is creation, in that humanity and the earth are so entwined. The ocean reaches our inmost being."

Chapter 14

Back in Lorain, Street Clubs

At the end of summer, after the recovery from the surgery, I was back in Lorain to fulfill my obligation to work for Catholic Charities for their help in sending me to school. I continued the same work as before, seeing some familiar Puerto Rican families and new ones. I worked with mentally disturbed families, broken families, elderly, and most every kind of human problem.

I walked and sat around in poor neighborhoods like South Lorain and the Campito. I continued to take Hispanic kids to Parmadale and help the nuns adjust to their new look. One very agile Puerto Rican boy slid down the drain from the third floor of a cottage at Parmadale, past the nun's room at night. The nun was ready to retire and she asked to leave. That was the beginning of the end. Today mostly lay people deal with that new breed of kid and the nuns continue their work in hospitals.

My spiritual life those days was centered in the Chapel of the Sacred Heart in South Lorain in that converted meat market, and in the Byzantine Catholic church nearby. My actual parish was St. Anthony's, a Franciscan church in Lorain, where I was now living, but I rarely went there.

My apartment was in an old brick building, and I had a third floor walk-up facing Lake Erie, giving me endless pleasure watching the water, the sunsets, the storms. It was as close to the ocean and Cape Cod as I could get in Ohio.

Sometimes I prayed for the boys and girls and families in my care, but mostly I just worked to make their life a little better, to talk with them, to visit them in jail or the detention home, to explain their behavior to teachers, to calm them when they were drunk. I knew their lives were the same as the lives I heard about from the men of skid row and the people in the V.A. hospital. Lost lives, comforted by alcohol. Alone. Someday many of them could be on skid row. What could I do to prevent this? I kept wondering.

Part of my job at Catholic Charities was with street groups, street gangs, who were fighting with one another over neighborhood territories, divided by races and nationalities and blocks of streets. The Chicanos were Mexican, and there were Puerto Rican groups, blacks, Appalachians, people from South Lorain, Central Lorain, the East Side. And whites-only groups.

John Dierna, my friend from Notre Dame, was the only county probation officer and we would talk a lot about the gangs. Once the judge wanted to send a whole group away to a state institution, but instead we talked. The judge decided to put them all on probation and in my care, or the care of the Lorain youth policeman. The boys could choose. He also made a condition that if any one got in trouble, all would be sent away. I never knew if he would have really done this, and I'm not sure he knew, but it was a strong threat.

The boys chose me to be their "advisor" and an idea was born, which is still part of my life: make a family-like group out of this gang, so they would have something, someone, to call their own, a new family. They had their street life in common. The one factor common to all the skid row and alcoholic tubercular V.A. people was weak family ties, often none at all, or downright hatred in families.

At that time gangs were a big thing in New York City, Chicago, other cities, and the solution for these others was to break them up, using street or gang social workers who would get to know them. Then the police would arrest the "psychotic" leaders and send them to jail for murder and drugs. Next they worked to send the fringe member hangers-on to trade school or into the military service. They did not worry about the largest number of gang followers in the middle, the biggest part of any gang, with no special skills for school or job training. They could go on welfare or drift around.

I visited programs doing this in New York City at The Henry Street Settlement House, at HARYOU (The Harlem Youth Project) in Harlem, the Blackstone Rangers in Chicago, and went to meetings and workshops to learn. Because of my interest, a contact was made with an Italian vice-mayor in New York City who took me to see gangs in the Bronx, Brownsville, Harlem, even a Jewish gang. We spent days in what seemed like bombed-out neighborhoods. There were whole blocks of rubble, with no standing buildings and scarcely anyone on the street.

I found out the authorities did succeed in breaking up the gangs, arresting the leaders and saving the hangers-on who had family ties. But the big group in the middle, now feeling abandoned and alone, turned to drugs. They introduced the drug culture into those cities. They had nothing except the drugs. The gangs had been holding them together, giving them meaning, life, purpose. Now that was gone. Their psychopathic gang leader father figures were in jail. Drugs filled the void, with their day and night buzz and high, and then the need to rob to get money to get high the next day. There was nothing to live for except this.

It was my perception that the original gangs served a partly good and vital purpose in the lives of the members, and they should be kept together to help one another, like a family or a social club.

There were a dozen members in that first court-approved group I met with in Lorain, and our first gathering was in a small apartment on South Lorain's Vine Avenue, the home of one of the boys. He lived above a bar. They did not trust me one bit, but they needed me to keep from getting sent away to the state.

We grew on one another. I wrote about them. The judge came to visit them. They bought jackets to show they were a club, a family of sorts. They went on as friends and supporters for years, and still see one another, almost 30 years later.

When the news broke on TV about my indictment and arrest, the first person to call that night was the original leader of this gang, and a few minutes later his best friend called from Florida, another member of the gang.

That concept of using the natural group, the group with common ties and problems, to help one another was the seed for Betterway's group homes, the foster homes, and later the adult homes for people with nowhere to live, the homeless, the people of the streets. They have something in common and can support and help one another, just like those gangs did.

I found a spiritual meaning in all this. God conceivably could have existed alone as one person, but it is the teachings of my religion and others, that God is somehow three persons, a father, a son, and the spirit of love between them, so strong that it is a third person. If this is true, then God is a social being, living with others, a trinity of persons.

If we are made in the image and likeness of our maker, then that explains why we too are social beings. We like to be around other people, to share with them. New life, a baby, come into being through an intimate social act between two people, and that baby is normally raised by those two people in a family, a small society, a trinity.

Our spirit and body cries out for others. We long to be sociable. We believe that a "loner" is somehow disturbed, mentally off balance.

I did not have these thoughts well articulated when I was starting the gangs and group homes, but the ideas were in the background. Somehow I knew the people of skid row, of gangs, of ghettos, could help one another by sticking together. I wanted to help that happen with my life.

Sickness entered my life yet again. My eye developed more problems and after a long time of medication and probing, the Cleveland surgeon I was now seeing decided to operate. It was the same kind of surgery I had in Boston and resulted in blurred vision in the left eye and the need for regular checkups the rest of my years.

This surgery, performed at Hanna Hospital in Cleveland was rare at the time and six younger doctors looked on. It was performed with a sedative numbing my face so I could move my eye during the surgery. I could also watch the scalpel cutting my eye, which was very nerve-wracking. And I watched the doctors watch me.

After it was over they put me to sleep and I remained in the hospital for some days.

It seemed like I had less and less control over my life.

Prayer

"Dear Lord, I returned to my home area and never left again. I got to know many people in my county with big and small problems. I also met those who were trying to solve their problems for them, and found that some just made things worse. Most, suffering, had the ability to solve their own problems with a tiny bit of help.

"I thank you for helping me see the strength in people, even when they seem down and out. Help me to always respect the needy, the poor."

Chapter 15

Gangs and Cursillos

The work with gangs of boys, and then their girl friends, took more and more of my time. I developed camping trips and outings to nearby cities and walks in the country, suited just to such gangs. I kept notes on what worked and what was boring. Most of the gangs became clubs, with rules and penalties, dues, officers, and activities.

I worked four years for Catholic Charities after my graduate degree and the gang work was now so prominent that the United Way people asked me to organize such groups full time in a new project they would fund. They were hiring me to do my own thing. It wasn't much of a change and I did it, and the Pilot Youth Project was born.

Chauncey Smythe was chairman of the United Way Board and we met for lunch at his Thew Shovel Company (then Lorain Crane) and shared enthusiasm. This wonderful local philanthropist entered my life a number of times later, including after his death.

I wrote my gang ideas in a booklet and called them VIA clubs, a Latin Word, meaning WAY, with the motto, "Help along the way." VIA also stood for Volunteers in Action. There were now so many boys and girls wanting clubs that I recruited volunteers to meet with them weekly. The adult acted as a helper, referee, and driver for activities, but did not run the group. Their own officers ran the group.

Soon there were so many volunteers I did not have much time to train them. About then VISTA came into existence as a national domestic Peace Corps. We got 19 of the first VISTA volunteers to go anywhere. I was in Washington getting them lined up before VISTA offices were fully open.

We had VISTA Volunteers living in pairs in poor Lorain neighborhoods, including Campito, working with the clubs and gangs in their area, and then with the families. The kids hung around the VISTA houses and this led to the idea for a group home. Our first group home was called VIA House.

Later we called it The Beacon Boys Home. This sounded more adventuresome and meaningful than VIA. Beacon meant a light, a beacon of hope in a storm, since we were near the lake. My boyhood friend, John Bazley, who had just finished 10 years at Parmadale, came to open that first group home. It turned out to be the first such home in the world for teenagers. Now group homes exist in many countries.

That was the beginning of Betterway. It did not go smoothly. We originally found a house on one street and were ready to open when the neighbors picketed the governor. There were no black people on their street, only at the end streets. We lost the fight but were offered a place in South Lorain by a Realtor, William Nicola. We really liked it better, since the area was more Hispanic and racially mixed.

There was a big public fight over the first home that we did not get, and I learned to be patient and to lay low, finding out that if we "lost" we would really "win" by getting public support. I have kept this in mind all my life in all my public battles.

During those years the Spanish people in Lorain were getting into something religious called The Cursillo, which meant, Little Course. It was a retreat-type movement conceived in Spain, going to South America, Mexico, and then into Texas, and across this country, but only in Spanish, and in Spanish neighborhoods.

The retreat began on a Thursday evening and ended Sunday night, at a ceremony-party called the Clausura, the Closing.

During the Cursillo, people slept very little. They talked a lot with one another in small table groups about their inner spiritual life, their feelings about Christ, how they helped other people, how they prayed. They learned to pray spontaneously, aloud, almost in a Pentecostal, born-again way, before those ideas were popular among Catholics.

The Closing or final event on Sunday night was attended by all the people who had made a Cursillo in the past from as far away as could come. There were sometimes hundreds of people, bursting in on the 20 or so in the new group, singing exuberantly in Spanish, hugging and laughing, seeming to me to be another foretaste of what heaven must be like. Many knew one another from the neighborhood or job, and many were strangers.

A follow-up meeting to the Cursillo experience was to be held weekly, with the table groups coming together to pray and discuss how they were doing in their spiritual life and their love of Jesus.

The Cursillo was a very intense experience, suited to the strong emotions of the Spanish person. There might be weeping, laughing, repenting, and sometimes nearly an emotional collapse.

I watched the Puerto Rican and Mexican men and then the women get involved in these Cursillos, but I did not know enough Spanish to attend and understand them. Then a priest in Cincinnati, a Franciscan we knew as Father Fidelis, began to give his version of a Cursillo in English. He had come from Texas and spoke Spanish, learning the Cursillo program there.

Msgr. Newton, still in my life these times, told me to go to Cincinnati and make the English Cursillo and bring it back to St. Mary's, his parish, in English.

I went to Cincinnati one extremely hot, muggy weekend, slept on cots in a gym with 50 other men, and was put through the wringer, spiritually and emotionally. Father Fidelis was excitable, like Father Mathis at Notre Dame. He jumped and shouted, wept and yelled, prayed and sang aloud, using all the emotions available. So did the team of men, "insiders," who also participate and help carry it all out, although the new participants do not know they are "insiders" until it is all over.

The insiders have been through other Cursillos and try to steer the new men and women to achieve a conversion of the heart. It is kind of a spiritual brainwashing technique, to break down formal religious feelings and barriers between people and God and people and people.

My life was not the same after that weekend. It was the 12th Cursillo to be held in English anywhere in the world.

My reserved, inner spirit, a love for the formal liturgy, was now supplemented outwardly by my emotions. I had looked down on emotions in religion. Religion was to be of the mind. I did have strong feelings on some of the feasts, with some of the music, and with some of the psalms, but I never showed this and never "hugged" in religion, and never prayed spontaneously aloud.

After my Cursillo I was bubbling over to show my religion and talk about Christ. Probably too much so, and in typical fashion I told everyone I knew about the Cursillo. Then we learned about a priest giving Cursillos in English in Kalamazoo, Michigan. I began to urge my friends to go there, including John Bazley.

We had a dozen men go to Michigan, enough local people for a team, and convinced the priest and his crew to come down to Ohio. We put on the first Cursillo in English in our parts in the old St. Paul's Protestant church, then belonging to St. Mary's, and since torn down. We had 17 men in our first Cursillo, including Msgr. Newton. Hundreds of Spanish people came from all over to attend the Closing, the most wonderful event of my life up to then.

It lasted all night it seemed, in a jammed hot basement of this former Lutheran church. That night I went home to my apartment, alone, exhausted, with a bag of money donated by the participants, each giving what they could, and I fell on the floor, the money spilling out. I tried to count it and got far enough to know we about broke even on expenses. I barely crawled into bed. We were not in debt. The Cursillo movement was underway in Northern Ohio.

Many more Cursillos for men followed, then some for women, then we went on to Erie, Pa., Syracuse, and other cities into the East coast. I was the director of most of them and was making up my own content and outline for the 12 talks. In the Cursillo format the talks were given by twelve different people, then discussed at length at each table, with the hope that the table would become a tightly knit group, helping one another to make changes and promises for a more active, alive religion. A person felt wrong not to go with the group, they felt separated. So they went along, hopefully willingly and happily, but not always.

Finally I needed to let others be the leaders and decided to put the oral talks down in written form. I decided against a literal translation of the Spanish, which was too formal in style for me. I got together with a priest from Puerto Rico, Father Antonio, and we took the original format and its ideas and put it into modern lay concepts. These were along the Catholic Action lines of Msgr. Reynauld Hillenbrand, and Dom Chautard in his classic, *The Soul of the Apostolate*.

Father Antonio and I did this at my house over a period of a few days, producing a Cursillo manual which some people assumed was a translation of the Spanish original. Our version was used everywhere for some years until some decided the movement had to get back to its "authentic" Spanish roots and did a literal translation.

My parting from the Cursillo movement came after three years as diocesan chairman for Cleveland, when I proposed that Protestants be able to be part of Cursillo weekends. This led to big debates about receiving Communion. Some said Communion was the heart of the Cursillo, and since Protestants could not receive Communion, they should not participate.

Protestants were already making Cursillos at Notre Dame and I knew it was going well. The Communion question was resolved by talking about it in advance with all the participants, and talking about the unity among people that still existed even though everyone did not receive Communion.

In any case, I used this refusal by the diocese as an excuse to step out of the movement. I was also worn out and looking for something new.

The "something new" came along in the form of the Gabriel Richard Leadership Institute. I became the director of this for two years, introducing this Christian version of a Dale Carnegie Course into the Cleveland area, as a kind of natural follow-up on the Cursillo. It helps people move from wanting to do something new to help society to actually doing it. It moves from resolve to action.

The Cursillo Movement is now a national program across the United States, and the Gabriel Richard Leadership Institute continues in some places.

During all of this Cursillo work I had my full-time job as a Social Worker with the street clubs.

Prayer

"De Colores!—the greeting between those who have made a Cursillo, The Little Retreat. De Colores: color your life with Jesus, with others.

"Lord, you sent the Cursillo into my life just when it was needed, like all the other happenings. You opened my spirits to others in ways I had never known. The Hispanic people will always be dear to me and I know, that they, like all people, reflect the way you are."

Chapter 16

Mexico, Guadalupe

In the heart of the Cursillo movement is a devotion to Our Lady of Guadalupe, the patron of Spanish speaking Catholics of the world, and especially of Mexico.

On December 9 in 1531 The Mother of Christ, Mary, appeared to an Indian Christian, Juan Diego, in Mexico, and told him to build a church on that spot in her honor. He was poor and lowly and the Bishop did not believe him, so Mary left her picture on his cloak. This image of a peasant-looking woman, convinced the Bishop and several large churches have been built there since then. Pilgrims go to Guadalupe from all over the world to see the cloak and the picture in a glass frame above the main altar. It is life sized.

The Cursillo often uses a hymn to Our Lady of Guadalupe to end the whole weekend and people sing it in Spanish over and over. This hymn is popular in all Spanish speaking churches.

There was a workshop on Cursillos in Texas and my friend John Bazley, then still at Parmadale, and active with the Cursillo, decided to go with me to Texas. We would go on to Mexico City and the shrine of Guadalupe.

The meeting in Texas had to do with the style of Cursillos and other ordinary matters, and people were interested in what we were doing to spread it East. It was not an exciting time in Texas. But Mexico was.

We were driving, it was hot, and by the time John and I got to Mexico City I was very sick and spent three days finding a doctor and medicine. It was the water, and I had been careless. My collapse came at the basilica of Guadalupe with thousands of pilgrims, and me laying in a dark corner of an outside wall, too sick to get up, staying there until I felt able to move to find a doctor.

When I recovered we went back to the shrine, a big Spanish looking church, with a block long plaza leading to the entrance. The plaza was paved with rough cobblestones. Devout Mexicans fell on their knees at the beginning of this plaza and crawled to the entrance of the church. They would go up the aisle, stopping directly in front of the altar and the picture of Our Lady of Guadalupe, still on their knees. A religious penance and a sign of veneration and humility.

It was a weekday when we returned after my illness. Not too many people were there and a wedding was ready to start inside the church. This is a favorite place for the wealthy to marry.

I was standing at the edge of the plaza a block from the church and some pilgrims were going slowly along on their knees and I suddenly felt compelled to get on my knees. The other pilgrims looked to be all Mexican peasants, poor people, probably in from the hills. I did not see any other Americans.

On my knees I went slowly across the plaza; I don't know how long it took. Another wedding was in progress when I reached the church, and I was in a daze, filled with emotions, sighing tears. I went up the aisle on my knees in front of any people that might be looking until I got before the picture. This was the first time I had seen it. I was overwhelmed. Joyful, humbled, forgetting the church full of people there for the wedding and forgetting the other pilgrims.

I stayed kneeling a long time. Mass went on in Spanish, people rejoiced over the married couple. I don't recall how I got up and left, but next I joined other pilgrims walking up the outside stairs to the highest tower of the basilica, a traditional walk. I don't remember what I did up there because I accidentally stepped on a young man who had no legs. He was moving up the stairs on his wooden platform with rollers underneath.

I felt so bad over stepping on him that I forgot everything else.

We returned to the church other times, but the main experience was over for me, and something had happened inside me.

I was a proud person, having been given due honor by lots of people those six years in the seminary. Even though I left, the aura remained. I was seminary trained. I was director of the Cursillo movement in our area. Kids and clients liked me. I spoke Spanish. I got good grades when I was in school and I was fairly smart. I could express myself in words and talks. The newspapers wrote about me. I wrote articles for the papers. I was somebody.

Crawling on my knees across the plaza with Mexican peasants had done something to my pride. I felt more a part of ordinary life, less aloof. Many of the images in the psalms speak of David as humbled, in the dust, a man of little status in the whole of creation, in the sight of God. In other biblical places, there is the phrase "I am a worm and no man." Later used by Jesus to describe his own condition at death.

Pride returned over the years, but events helped keep me humble, more than I ever planned.

The result of the trip to Texas and Mexico was a deepened devotion to Our Lady of Guadalupe, and a lessening of some of my pride.

We also toured around the poor areas. We found a priest to take us into the compounds where dozens of families lived in one room doorless mud huts in a closed-in yard. Chickens and pigs were running around, a woman under a canopy at one end was cooking tortillas, the only food. These families lived their lives here. When the kids got to be eight or nine the aggressive ones left to make it on their own, sleeping in the town plazas, selling gum to tourists, stealing.

The poverty I saw was beyond comprehension in our country and yet there was a joy among the people, and even among the homeless kids, who formed into groups to help one another to grow up. A familiar idea.

The poor of our country never seemed so poor after that.

When I returned home I was ready to let others into my life, which led to marriage and an instant family.

Prayer

"Next you brought Mary, the Mother above all mothers, into my life in a new way. I had always liked May Devotions. I liked to visit the shrines of Mary in my travels, but going to Guadalupe was very special, combined with moving on my knees with the peasant people. You were breaking down my pride."

OUR LADY
of Guadalupe

Chapter 17

Marriage, a Honeymoon to Chicago, Mexico Again

I had fallen in love four times in my life, once in high school, again between seminary times with a Mexican woman, again when at Catholic Charities with an Italian, and in Boston with a Boston woman and her little girl. But none of these love friendships resulted in marriage. I think I was too filled with my own importance to accept anyone as an equal or to let them enter into my inner personal life.

After returning from Mexico, and with my involvement in the Cursillo, my feelings were more open. One day a neighbor boy asked me to come watch him play basketball in his grade school league. I did, and then took him and his best friend home. The best friend told me his father was dead and I felt sorry for him, the social worker in me. I took him and his brother and sister a few places, met their mother, started taking the family out. A year later I was in love with Mary, their mother, going back and forth every night from my apartment in Lorain to be with them in Elyria.

The woman was Mary Francis Toby Bradley and she had married in Louisiana, a serviceman from the Air Base, near her home in DeRidder, La. They moved to Elyria, near his home in Grafton, Ohio. They had a baby boy, then twins, a boy and girl. "Brad" got cancer and died shortly after, leaving Mary with the three babies. She looked into welfare and decided it was better to work, so her sisters came up from Louisiana and helped watch the kids and she raised them to the ages they were now, 12 and 15.

One day I realized I could not live without this family in my life and I asked Mary to go to Mass with me on a Saturday at Sacred Heart Chapel in Lorain, that converted meat market.

There was that big life-sized replica of the picture of Our Lady of Guadalupe on a side area of the chapel. After Mass, in front of this shrine, I asked Mary to marry me. We had talked about this a few days earlier, so it was no surprise. (Some years later this building was torn down, a handsome new Spanish style chapel built, and the picture relegated to a ceiling storage area. On a tour one day I spotted it and asked for it, and it now hangs in a meeting room at the Betterway farm).

We planned a big wedding for April 4, 1964, (celebrating our 25th. anniversary in the year of my trial).

The three kids weren't sure they wanted me as a father, a friend was alright, but fathers could be strict. They got over these feelings and had a good time with it all.

Msgr. Newton had the wedding. An all black club, the Sahieves, acted as ushers, and the church was filled with friends, mostly from the Cursillo, many Hispanic. By this time Mary had made a Cursillo and was part of the movement.

The wedding was sensational, people singing the songs I had rewritten for the Cursillo from traditional songs, like, "When The Saints Go Marching In," "America the Beautiful," "Swing Low Sweet Chariot." At the end a Mexican friend sang the Guadalupe song with his guitar and everyone joined in, "Adios O Virgen de Guadalupe." Everybody cried, shouted, and clapped. At the end Monsignor told me, "Now that's the way to get married."

Our best man and matron of honor, Mime and Bob O'Donnell, lifelong friends, told us to make our first honeymoon stop at a motel in Toledo. It turned out to be part of the criminal world, probably the Mafia, and the room next to ours, with a thin wall, was used by two prostitutes. Their customers got robbed in the process that night. We stayed awake, ready to duck the bullets that might come through the wall. The other side of our room was a glass wall, facing the indoor recreation

Mary and I cutting our wedding cake which was made by friends and fed the several hundred people at our reception.

area. This had a pool table, and swimming pool. Echoing pool balls and diving people splashing into the water filled the air. This also went on all night and into the morning. We ended up laughing at this honeymoon spot.

The next day we drove on to South Bend and a motel in the sight of Notre Dame. We walked around the campus and found peace. I had already taken my instant family into this part of my life, so Notre Dame was not new for Mary.

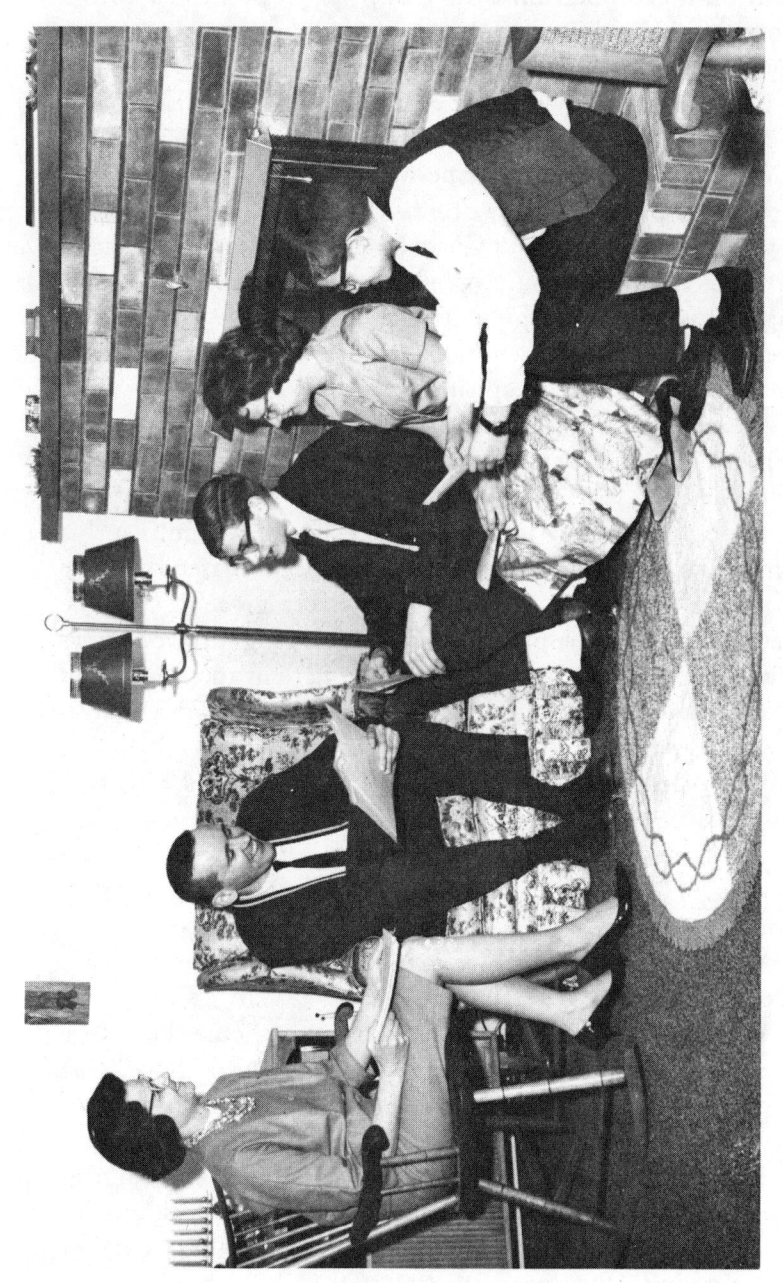

My instant and wonderful new family, Mary, and the 3 kids, Tom, Pam, and Don. We were sitting by the fireplace of our new home.

We went on to Chicago where we had reservations in an old, high ceilinged hotel on Ohio Street, appropriately. It was a wonderful Victorian hotel, not restored, low cost, almost musty. But somehow just right.

For years Mary had supported the National Shrine of St. Jude in Chicago and prayed to St. Jude to get through life, so we had decided to visit this shrine while we were there.

With help from a map we found the church. To our surprise, it was named Our Lady of Guadalupe. The National Shrine to St. Jude was in the Church of Our Lady of Guadalupe in Chicago. This was like a sign to us that our marriage was made in heaven, since the two devotions in our lives were here as one. Kind of corny, but also spiritual.

We enjoyed Chicago and headed home uneventfully. We began to plan a long trip in my station wagon to Mexico, back to Guadalupe, with the five of us.

We made the trip, and Mexico did not make me sick this time as I took medicine and was careful of the water, drinking mainly cold cerveza, beer. The kids had a great time at the markets, getting the prices down, and we caught the two boys with cigarettes when they thought we were in another part of the market. Being caught red-handed in Mexico with contraband was a blow to their youthful cunning.

We visited the Guadalupe shrine and lots of cities, including some of the poor areas again, this time with a priest who was living there from Cincinnati. It got very hot and we all got sick crossing a desert area. The station wagon was not air conditioned.

We made it back in Elyria with rich memories to last a lifetime.

When we got married we bought a new house, built by a friend, in a newly developing area of Elyria and have lived there ever since. It is six blocks from the house I lived in at birth, 10 blocks from the hospital where I was born.

During these years my spiritual life centered on the Cursillo, the small group meetings called reunions, the Byzantine Church, and a new parish in Elyria, Sacred Heart of Jesus. This was a mainly Hungarian church, built in 1929, but now in a small neighborhood where black people lived. Few went to church there of any race, when a bright young priest was assigned to the place to be a Newman chaplain at Oberlin College and the new Lorain County Community College. A number of people were attracted to his contemporary preaching. A young musician, writing his own church music, started attending there, and this developed into a so-called non-territorial parish, one open to anyone, regardless of where they lived. The musician was Joe Zsigray, he had been in the seminary a short time and hung around Betterway a lot.

Sacred Heart in Elyria is still the parish of our choice, although the original priest and two others since then have moved on in their careers.

Prayer

"Lord, you sent Mary the Mother of Jesus to me, and now another Mary came into my life. I thank you for this ready-made family. They have been a steady delight on my journey. Mary has meant more to me than any other person I have known. Thank you for giving us to one another."

Chapter 18

Betterway Grows, and Grows, and Grows.

It is a little difficult for me to see my spiritual journey in the growth of Betterway, but it is there.

I felt driven to take people into my life, under my care, when they were having troubles. I put some in Parmadale Children's Village before I had any places of my own. I was not happy with Parmadale for these kids, as the place was geared to the well behaved, not allowing for the talents and spontaneity of many of the boys and girls I had. I had led my lifelong friend, John Bazley, into Parmadale to work so he could add his human touch to what I thought was too strict an atmosphere. For instance, everyone had to attend Mass and to kneel upright with no meaningful explanation of any of this for those who were not Catholic.

When we got the idea of opening a "place of our own" with a group home in the community I was excited. The Beacon was opened October 7, 1966.

I could not take these kids into my personal life at home, but I did create a home for them, a real home like I wanted them to have, instead of the large institutions where I had been taking them.

A year after the Beacon was opened, the state asked us to create a similar home for girls and we found an available large home in Elyria belonging to some friends. They also owned a small Catholic religious goods store in a concrete block building added on to the front of their house. It was along Middle Avenue, a busy street in downtown Elyria. It was called Bornino's Religious Goods. They were Joe and Enza Bornino.

They wanted to end the religious goods business, which was doing poorly, and move to California, so they offered it all to us cheaply. In 1968 we opened a group home for girls, and our own shop. We let the first three girls choose a name, and they thought up "The Search" saying they had been searching for a home for years. One had come from an institution, one was a prostitute, one from a bad home.

We liked the name so much we used it for the store too, The Search Shop. We kept some of the religious articles and added items of all faiths, including Jewish and Mormon. We added regular gift items and books, especially for Elyria High School across the street.

The idea of a book or gift shop was not new for me. At St. Charles College I was involved in opening a small bookstore for students and faculty. This led me to getting the names and

A happy moment with one of the Betterway girls who graduated and was off to a dinner at the school. Graduation at Betterway from Elyria High School was not common, but one year 7 boys and girls succeeded in doing so.

The Beacon Home for Boys in its third and final location. The Betterway office is next door. All our homes were restored and painted in original colors.

addresses of publishers, learning wholesale buying, reading reviews, returning unsold books. At St. Mary's Seminary I added a large pamphlet selection to their book selling. At St. Mary's parish in Elyria I operated a small shop of religious articles in the basement during the years I worked there.

The new part at The Search Shop for me was the addition of gifts of a general nature, and regular books. Some years later we moved the girls home out to make room to expand the store into selling jeans, shirts, and natural foods, sort of a 60's "hippie" shop, also with posters, to attract young people and the otherwise alienated. It worked well, but some years later yet we needed the space for girls again. The jeans business was too competitive, and grocery chains started carrying natural foods, so we dropped those items and restored the home. Over the years our primary sales are still in religious goods, including candles, cards, church bulletins, and some other supplies. For a long time we were the only religious goods store in Elyria.

We have sold over a million dollars in religious goods in our community, from penny "holy pictures" to high priced bibles and art work. We also gave out free copies of The Catholic Worker newspaper.

Shortly after opening the Search Shop and Home we had problems with the community again in Lorain, some neighbors feeling our Beacon boys were responsible for problems in

A Betterway boy's home on one of the many trips to the Smoky Mountains. Pictured with an Indian in Cherokee, North Carolina.

South Lorain. We decided to move our Beacon Home to Elyria so the two homes would be close and easier to run. We found a big house a block away from the Search and rented there for 10 years, until it was torn down. The beginnings of the office of Betterway were in that large old Victorian place, falling apart, but beautiful inside. The owner never wanted to fix it up.

Next we added a home for men coming out of prison. It was named The Bridge. Some of the new men had been former residents of our boys home and needed a place to go. We could not take them back since our Beacon home was licensed for juveniles, so an adult place came along naturally. I still wanted to take in all these I knew who needed a place.

The adult home went well and the state asked us to open a pilot program for men coming out of prison prior to parole, a pre-release program. We bought another house, across from the Search, and opened that for a year calling it The Anchor. But the state had too many problems with this type program in another city and under strong legislative criticism, ended the concept for awhile. We had an empty house.

Some of our youths were doing poorly in regular public school and we raised the funds to open an alternative school for 17 of them in this empty house. Some students were from our homes, some the problem kids from the nearby high school. It pleased the school to get these kids out of their hair, and surprised the school when they did well. This made for good cooperation between us and the school. We ran that program for three years until our relationship with the school was so good that our boys and girls no longer needed a separate place and the house became a second boys group home.

During these years I ended my work with street groups in Lorain, and the Pilot Youth Project became a regular agency in the county, Youth Services Inc., offering mostly drug related counseling and still working with some of the street groups. However, the era of gangs was passing and this work was not needed. Youth Services changed its name several times and still exists, offering a wide variety of services, being the major private youth serving agency in Lorain County. It has no connection to Betterway other than its beginning.

When the Pilot Youth Project ended, I took a job at The Cleveland Foundation as a day-by-day consultant. That turned into my work for the next three years, while I also ran Betterway and did some teaching at Cleveland State University.

Prayer

"Lord, now the next chapter in my life unfolded: Betterway, and thousands of young people who came to live in my world. I did not know that one day they would consume me, overwhelm me. At first there were just 11 boys, then 11 girls, then hundreds. Then men coming from prison. Then more.

"I came to know almost everyone. I never met anyone I did not like, no matter what they were. I could see your reflection in each, although sometimes it was only a glimpse of goodness, the rest hidden by the poisons of the circumstances in their lives.

"I am grateful for all those lives, and look forward to seeing them again, too."

Chapter 19

The Cleveland Foundation: The Cleveland Scene

The Cleveland Foundation was the first community foundation in the world. These differ from family and corporation foundations. Foundations are set up to give money to government approved charities, schools, and churches to do works that benefit society. Wealthy families and corporations set up foundations, with government approval, to lessen the taxes they would otherwise pay. But it takes a fair amount of family or corporate money to do this and a man in Cleveland got the idea of people pooling their money to create a "community" foundation. The board would be appointed by local government and by banks. The banks would invest the pooled money and the interest would be given away, just like families and corporations performed.

The Cleveland Foundation started in 1914 and the idea spread. By the time I came on the scene they had pooled a lot of money in Cleveland and were funding programs in the youth field. They wanted to work with street groups like I had done in Lorain, and they wanted to involve the city and the schools in carrying out the work.

After talking with me, Dr. James (Dolph) Norton, the director, asked me to come to Cleveland and set up a program for youth in trouble, the boys and girls to be identified by the schools, and the program run by the city out of city hall, using volunteers to be trained by Cleveland State University. The Youth Program Development Project eventually came from this idea and did many things.

I was given an office at city hall under the nation's first big city black mayor, Carl Stokes, and later under mayor Ralph Perk. I got to know the city well. I found out that thousands of dollars were being given to youth programs by at least 25 family and corporate foundations and other government agencies, but no one coordinated the funding or the programs, so no one knew what anyone was doing in the various neighborhoods of the city.

It was my job to organize the funding, private and government, and then organize the services. The programs had to work together to serve kids if they wanted any money. We held many meetings for hundreds of agency people and other meetings for the funding people and things did come together. We drew in millions of dollars in Federal Neighborhood Youth Corps job funds, increasing the Cleveland kids working in summers from 3,000 to 12,000. We coordinated all funds and jobs and programs by neighborhoods. After three years the work was taken over by the Federation for Community Planning. I was also an adjunct associate professor at Cleveland State, teaching in Social Service.

I returned to Betterway full time after three years.

I learned about the sources of money and worked with the wealthy of Cleveland, the individuals and the companies, Vernon Stouffer, the Schuberts, the McMillans, the Holdens, and all the major corporations. Teaching at Cleveland State took me into the workings of an inner city university, struggling in its views about admitting black students. Blacks were half the population of the city.

I learned a lot about politics. Carl Stokes drew visitors from around the world and reshaped Cleveland's politics to include black people. I saw unbelievable political uses of millions of dollars, decisions made in closed rooms. Once during a major decision-making meeting, two men excused themselves, went to another room, and the one hit the other over the head with a table leg, sending him to the hospital. Compromise in the big city.

I had two places where I went to find God. One spiritual oasis was the Cathedral of St. John, a few blocks from where I worked. Big, Gothic-American, with street people often sleeping in the back pews on cold days and hot days. Hundreds of people would be at noon Mass and again at 5 p.m. The church had lots of side altars and carved statues and candles and was peaceful.

The other oasis was a chapel called St. Paul's, near Cleveland State, still in downtown Cleveland, where the Franciscans held perpetual adoration of the Blessed Sacrament, the bread we believe is Christ. It is displayed day and night in a gold and glass container for the public to see above the main altar. I went there when I could and pondered this mystery, how it could be, believing it by faith, and some understanding.

Sometimes I would also walk down to Lake Erie, just behind Cleveland's city hall, and again find God in water, the waves, the vastness of the sea. Lake Erie is 30 miles across and looks endless, like the ocean.

During those years I was also a member of the Commission on Catholic Community Action, a new social action arm of the Cleveland diocese, meeting regularly in downtown Cleveland. I was there from its beginning, along with the priest representative of the diocese, Bishop William Cosgrove. After his retirement he became my spiritual director and counselor during the difficult times of my life. By then he had retired to live in a parish in Elyria, near the family of his brother.

At these commission meetings I met lay people and priests and nuns who were very bright, tuned in to the problems of racism, poverty, education, war. It was refreshing to find these people, and even better when I found they could create and enjoy the same kinds of liturgy I liked. They were "my kind of people," and had been there all along.

At the university I taught some young students but also people already in the work world, policemen, firemen, social workers. The social service department had offices on the 17th. floor of a tower building, overlooking the lake, which could be seen through a tiny window.

I have always enjoyed teaching, trying to sit the class in a circle to keep everyone alert and to get everyone to participate and get to know one another. I try to make a group out of the class so they help each other.

That is part of my group orientation: clubs, homes, classes, and counseling too. I like to do group counseling whenever I can. It helps people to realize they are not alone with their problem, and they get ideas from each other for solutions.

I often rode to my big city job in Cleveland on the Greyhound from Elyria, which was another group experience. The same people took the bus every day, an hours ride each way. Any new face was like a stranger stepping into a family living room.

Spiritually, the Cleveland experience broadened my outlook on humanity, and helped me find kindred souls.

One of the last things I did at the Cleveland foundation was take a trip to Europe to visit and write about youth-related programs.

Prayer

"Cleveland was the "big city" of my growing-up days. I would take the bus to see the sights, the movies, the theatre shows. I loved to visit the cathedral, the shrine of St. Paul's where the Eucharist was always shown, the big stores. And now I was working back in that downtown.

"I loved the street preachers, the street people. It was a bit of Chicago all over, but only 25 miles from home. I also came to know the wealthy, the rich people and the politicians. I found good in them, too. They were as good as anyone else, and had their poisons, too.

"Thank you for broadening my world some more."

Chapter 20

Europe

Mary and I went to Europe in the Fall of 1975. My expenses were paid by the Cleveland Foundation. We went on a Scandinavian Air Lines, waiting in the terminal in New York City next to a group going to Italy. Our group of passengers were reserved and quiet. The Italians, noisy, and lively. We almost wished we were going to Italy.

Our purpose was to visit group homes, runaway shelters, prisons, alcohol and drug programs, psychiatric hospitals, anything relating to youth and human services, and adult corrections. Through the Cleveland International Program we had a personal connection in each country, plus knowing some people who had come to see Betterway over the years.

We started our tour in Oslo, the capital of Norway and were taken around by a psychiatric social worker, a woman who had visited us. It was strange to see so many blond-headed people, tall, almost stately. Everyone looked alike to us. The Norwegian king's palace is in the heart of the city, and we watched "the changing of the guard" for the first time. We visited an alcohol treatment house, looking out on a city park next door, filled with Eskimos getting drunk. Skid row, in Norway.

We visited a runaway shelter filled with teenagers just like the ones we know, some being Eskimo boys and girls from remote villages. The parents were alcoholics. Or it was just a case where the lure of the big city led them to run. Most returned to their homes.

We spent a day at a psychiatric facility for children where the whole family comes to live each weekend, including grandparents, dogs, cats, birds, all joining the sick youth for group counseling.

In Stockholm, Sweden, we had a small hotel room in the heart of the city, by the water. We went to a concert in a state church, more like an ornate theater with lots of gold, and a royal box for the king and queen. A social worker who spent a summer at Betterway was our host.

We visited a prison where all the men went out to work each weekday and we went to a halfway house run almost like our Bridge Home. In Denmark we met more people we already knew, and they arranged for us to stay in an apartment in Copenhagen in a busy neighborhood. These friends, from India, took us to an old prison. When we finished our tour, the smiling warden pulled an immense curtain aside, revealing a 60 foot-high crucifix, Christ on the cross, looking down on the indoor prison courtyard, surrounded by five floors of cells. It was startling, and the warden said it was exposed for Sunday services, Protestant and Catholic.

We spent half a day in Copenhagen at a big commune called Christiani, where hundreds of young adults from all over Europe, many with children, have simply settled in. It is on the grounds of a former military camp, in the heart of Copenhagen, and these wandering people have their own school, dining hall, and tents and shacks and houses. The government authorities stay outside, including the police. As evening came on we walked in woodsy areas, across streams. People were cooking on outside fires, sitting around talking, in little clusters everywhere. It was fascinating to me. Uncounted hundreds of people lived at Christiani. It was an anarchist's dream world.

We were on our own in Amsterdam, Holland, missing a personal connection. We found the Van Gogh museum a wonder, as was storefront prostitution. The women were sitting in store windows looking like mannequins, dressed in Victorian clothing, perfectly still, with a wink now and then, and a beckoning finger to come in for business. Police were vigilant to see that the women did not set foot outside the "store" to attract customers. That is illegal.

Paris was our favorite European city. We stayed in a small French hotel on the island in the Seine where the city started, a block from Notre Dame Cathedral. The Isle de Cite where my Wimmers relatives may have lived. The island, with several famous bridges is packed with life, all surrounding the plaza and this magnificent church.

The narrow streets and old buildings hide the church until one comes right on it. We discovered it from the rear, with French mothers and children playing on the lawn. Like a post card. The stone flying buttresses, holding the walls up, are the most famous in the world and their beauty had me in tears. I had seen pictures but had no idea of their delicacy and size and the wonder of the whole structure. Some few sights in the world are breathtaking, and this the Cathedral of Notre Dame, the heart of Paris, is one.

Every day in Paris we found ourselves criss-crossing Notre Dame, in the morning, in the day, and at night. Visitors from all over the world mingle, sing, party, gape, climb the steps, and enter to hear the music, smell the incense, see the candles, the rich services, especially weddings. The river reflects the church, doubling the sight. At the far end of this plaza is one of the city's main jails and police stations. Such a contrast.

We loved the Latin Quarter of Paris, filled with students, visitors, Parisians, so many sidewalk cafes, filled with lookers and lookees in the early evening, after work. The name comes from the University in the area, where students studied Latin.

We stumbled onto small and large churches I had heard about, some with the great organs where my recordings of Bach were made.

One Saturday night the Latin Quarter Paris streets were full of people, packed, with musicians, jugglers, fire-eaters, sword swallowers, food, and mimes. We took it all in. Then we came on a small church on Avenue San Germaine, the church by the same name, which I had heard of. We went inside and someone was in the balcony playing Bach, a single candle burned before the altar, otherwise it was all dark. We went out

Notre Dame in Paris. I took this picture our first afternoon in that wonderful city. This was a view from the back, showing the flying buttresses, which held up the walls of this great Gothic cathedral.

and back in several times just to experience it. Outside was all that night revelry.

We could have stayed for weeks in Paris. We did get to the Louvre, the Eiffel Tower, at the end of the Chez Elysee, a wonderful wide avenue of shops and restaurants, Napoleon's silent, immense indoor tomb, so cold, so empty, was strangely fascinating.

We took a train to a port city, crossed the English channel and headed for London where we met more friends who had visited us in Elyria, a juvenile judge and his wife. We stayed a few days with them at their house in Wimbledon, and then at the Royal Horse Guards hotel across from Buckingham Palace, just to be in that area.

We were taken to Old Bailey, the most famous court in England, and sat in on the trial of The Seven, seven young people who picketed and distributed leaflets at an army base to protest war. One of the seven was the Cadbury son, the chocolate people, and he had a famous attorney, (a barrister) Louis Blum-Cooper, who took us to lunch and talked about the case. He is England's F. Lee Bailey. Lunch was in a small stand-up restaurant across from Old Bailey.

We walked around the great churches of London for hours, listened to some Episcopal monks chant Vespers at St. Pauls, and thought about the days when Henry VIII led his country away from being Roman Catholic to his own new state religion. We visited the Tower of London which was part of that religious revolution, Thomas More and all.

The next day we visited a Borstal, a boys reform school, and I talked to boys there, one telling me proudly that he was a "Borstal Boy." They had done the same kinds of things to get in trouble as our boys at Betterway. They had the same family stories.

We visited the world's first halfway house and a probation office. The halfway house opened in 1935 for men, and a few years later one opened next door for women. We walked under a big bridge; every inch of space had blankets and boxes, reserving the spot for individual homeless people to sleep that night. Reservations were necessary.

On our last night in Europe we had dinner with the juvenile judge and his wife at a hundreds of years old restaurant on the Thames, on Clink street, where the first jail or clink, was opened in London. Many people had eaten in this restaurant, back to the days of Shakespeare, Boswell, and Johnson.

We walked along Clink Street; the river was foggy, chilly, a scene from Dickens, a perfect ending.

The trip to Europe deepened my view of the world with its joys and miseries. It made history more real. There were so many religious and spiritual experiences that it is difficult to fit them in years later.

Overall, I came to appreciate even more the wonder of

people, the creativity of people in art and music and architecture, the beauty of this earth, even a chocolate pastry, and the greatness of the Lord in providing so much for our enjoyment.

Prayer

"You led me into yet another part of our world: Europe. The birthplace of my ancestors, the fascination of many of my studies.

"We found many famous churches and fell in love with the city of Paris and Notre Dame Cathedral. I wept when I saw it. I had studied the architecture at the University of Notre Dame and it seemed so magnificient, such an inspired work of art. I love your temples, O Lord."

Chapter 21

Canada

Another memorable one-of-a-kind trip, this one to Canada: Combermere, Ottawa, Montreal, Quebec, the Gaspé Peninsula and Acadian country, Nova Scotia, New Brunswick, and home through Maine. Seeing Combermere was our main purpose, the place founded by Catherine DeHueck Doherty and her husband Eddie.

Mary and I got our maps ready and headed out for Canada, through Niagara Falls, always a wonder to behold, and the long ride to Combermere, Ontario, in the middle of a wooded wonderland. I mentioned this place in my Chicago memories, and wrote of Catherine De Hueck Doherty, the Baroness. Combermere, a tiny town, is the place where she and her friends settled, on a river, to make their headquarters to train lay Catholics to work in poor areas around the world, as in their Friendship Houses. They called this place Madonna House.

When we got there the place was so crowded we had to stay in the only motel in the area, a small one down the road. Madonna House is like a big camp, where over 100 men and women live a fairly primitive Christian life, some staying permanently to form a core group, others remaining only a few months for training. In some ways it was like Grailville, but this was for men and women.

A group of core staff called "directors" meet almost daily in the early afternoon to make decisions on work, repairs, construction, meals, and all that goes into life when 125-150 people stay in one place.

Down the way a few miles they have a big farm, raising and drying herbs, making cheese from their own cows milk, raising chickens for eggs, and growing other food in a large garden. In another area there are a dozen log cabins, big enough for one person. Individuals can stay in them alone for a few days, taking a bible and a little bread and tea. This is a Russian concept for a retreat and is called a Poustinia.

Some people are frightened by large groups of people living together since they have bad ideas of cults, communes, Jonestown. But if the people want it to work out, it can, and the permanent leaders make it happen. One retired colorful archbishop of the Eastern Catholic rite lives there in a small house, and there are about seven priests to serve the community for confessions and liturgy.

Meals are simple, eaten in a large dining room, everyone taking turns helping prepare the food or clean up after the meal. Showers are primitive, taken once a week. Laundry is done in a central building. People sleep in large dormitories. It is almost like a monastery. There did not seem to be any married couples.

The chapel is almost circular, made from logs, a copy of a Russian peasant style, the favorite of Catherine. There are no pews or kneelers and people can choose for themselves whether to sit or kneel or squat or stand for prayers and liturgy. The services have a Russian Eastern Rite flavor, especially if the archbishop presides.

Catherine lived in a small log cabin near the church and was dying when we were there. She did die a few months later, but her spirit lives on and Madonna House goes on.

We met some women who were getting ready to go to London to open a place for retreats and to serve the poor in that city. Some others were going to Paris, and one woman had been in Cleveland, on the East side in a small store turned into a Poustinia.

The ideas of the Catholic Worker and Dorothy Day and

Peter Marin float around in this place: a return to the land, a simple life, serving poor people in cities, living together. Dorothy Day and Baroness DeHueck were close friends.

We could have stayed longer and did get a lot of ideas for Betterway, for the farm, for a community life someday, perhaps a community of misfits, down and out, and those not so. We also built a hut, a Yurt, at our farm, for the Poustinia idea (a Yurt is a small portable hut used by Nomads in the African desert).

We went on to Ottawa, the capital of Canada, seeing the government buildings and and the Rideau Canal, the waterway many use to skate to work in the winter. We were caught up by a rock and roll preaching group in a blue-green tent on the capital grounds, playing loud music and urging tourists to repent.

We liked Montreal more than Ottawa, with its French atmosphere, and did a lot of walking in the old downtown, finding a Cathedral that was bright gold and green inside and an even brighter chapel where Mass was going on in French. We stayed.

We drove up a hill to St. Joseph's Oratory, an immense church built with the efforts of a quiet man, a Holy Cross Brother, Andre, the doorman at the local college. He collected money for years and built this huge place. I knew a lot about him because I was in the same community, the Holy Cross Fathers.

We found the little room where Brother Andre lived his humble, nobody life, now crowned with this building looking down on all of Montreal, and visible from everywhere in the city. He left his mark.

Next, down the St. Lawrence River, was Quebec, even more French. We found a tiny room in a hotel overlooking the grand Chateau de Frontenac, a green jewel in the day and lit at night to catch the fancy.

Quebec sits on a cliff over the wide St. Lawrence, the prettiest city in Canada, like San Francisco, Boston, Paris, a magical city of beauty and people. Horses and buggies take visitors through the old walled city where we were. The sight from the city up on the cliff to the water below is spectacular any time of day or night.

We found Quebec to be a Catholic city, and went to Mass in a small church, highly decorated inside in all gold. It was a block from our hotel. We had the second best meal on the trip in a small Argentinian restaurant run by some people of Russian background.

Quebec is an "ode to joy" city, a celebration of life, with the streets filled day and night with artists, performers and tourists, from around the world.

We drove down the St. Lawrence to the church of St. Anne de Beaupre, the mother of the Blessed Virgin Mary. This is a major shrine in Canada like Guadalupe in Mexico. We went to Mass there and wandered the church and grounds, wishing it was a big feast day so there would have been a filled church and colorful liturgy. Hundreds of canes and crutches hang from pillars, testifying silently to miracles and cures.

For the next days we drove north along the St. Lawrence, ever widening until it looked like a lake, not a river, up into the green, French Gaspé Peninsula. We found the Acadian country, where the Canadians were from who went to Louisiana and were called Cajuns (Canadian Indians). We found names Mary knew from her home area, in an abandoned cemetery along the Gaspé, sitting among boulders washed in by the sea. Cities and towns had French names and big churches.

We went to Sunday Mass in Gaspé, a city at the tip of the land, and could not understand the English of the French-Canadian priest. We stopped for the night at a little seaside town and were directed to the Independence Restaurant on the beach, a diner-like little place. They were playing Bach on a stereo and serving the very best meal of the trip. What a surprise, and with the waves outside our window. It was a tiny, inexpensive restaurant.

We were now in the area of the high tides. At Moncton the river goes dry at low tide, and water comes in with a small wall as the tide reverses itself. It was even higher at the Bay of Fundy later.

We crossed the bridge into Nova Scotia, New Scotland, with

its Scottish population, staying at Halifax and seeing our first young people with the strange haircuts, and orange, green, yellow hair. Punk rockers. We got a kick out of them, and they were exuberant all night, like young people all over the world.

We stayed at a beautiful, quaint fishing town called Digby on the Bay of Fundy. We had a room on the third floor of a house, facing a stormy ocean. A few days later we were crossing the bay in a boat on a very stormy day when almost everyone got seasick. We stayed at St. Johns in New Brunswick a few days, then we headed into Maine.

In Canada we had the experience of a nearly all Catholic country in the Gaspe and Quebec areas, almost a state religion. Different from the Scandinavian countries where the state religion was Protestant. There is a feeling of comfort in having one's own religion all around.

Prayer

"Canada. So near, and yet I never came to know it until we made our big trip there. Again, we found such beautiful churches and scenery. We love the national shrine outside Quebec, St. Anne de Beaupre' and St. Joseph's Oratory in Montreal. St. Joseph's was built through the efforts of Brother Andre, a member of the Holy Cross Community, where I was a member for two years. We knew all about the humble Brother Andre and this immense basilica.

"We went to Combermere, founded by Baroness DeHueck, also from my past. We loved the Gaspé peninsula with its French population, the home of the Cajun people who live in Mary's Louisiana.

"O Lord, you were so good to us allowing us to see the wonders of Canada."

Chapter 22

Back to Betterway: The Deli, the Farm, the Trolley, New Programs

During the next years at Betterway, there were a number of high points. In 1974 we got the idea for a restaurant. It would be run by some of the people at Betterway. At that time we had a home for men coming out of prison and thought it would be a good project for them.

A small health food restaurant went out of business in a location on the downtown Elyria square. The place had been an eatery of different sorts for many years, being near the county courthouse and attorneys. We took it over and had the Bridge halfway house men renovate it into a Deli seating 65 people and also geared for carry-out business.

I also had in mind the idea of eating as an especially noble human act. Eating and sharing a meal is a major sort of interaction. The Catholic liturgy of the Mass is based on a meal, a sacred Jewish ceremony, the Passover meal. To give it a "Deli look" we hired a local Jewish woman to make her "famous" matzo ball soup and we served a few Kosher items. Matzo ball soup contains dumplings made from unleavened bread in a chicken broth.

For me there is something spiritual about a meal. We tried

to make the meal a high point in our life in the group homes. The Deli went on for 14 years, with little change in the menu, adding a hot dog wagon and later a popcorn wagon on the front sidewalk in warm weather. These were operated by Betterway youth, bringing us to the public eye and letting people ask questions about us.

The Deli was not part of the new adult Betterway programs as it became too costly to operate. It was sold in 1990 and is now an Italian eatery.

1976 saw the beginning of the Betterway newspaper, published with stories and pictures of youth and staff, printing 20,000 per issue after 10 years. All prisons and juvenile institutions in the United States received our paper. Some articles have been reprinted by others.

In 1979 Betterway acquired a farm property 15 miles south of Elyria in Wellington, Ohio. We bought 250 acres with a house, barn, and pond. Later we sold 100 acres to reduce the loan. The owners were Hungarian and among those people who founded Sacred Heart Church in Elyria, our parish. We did not intend to have a big farm, but mostly a place in the country for a garden and camping and retreats. One hundred acres is wooded land in gentle hills with a creek meandering through it all. The remainder of the land is lawn, a new five acre lake, and some tillable land rented to area farmers.

The idea of buying such a property had been with me since visiting the farm of the women at Grailville, reading the Peter Maurin Catholic Worker ideas, and reading the encyclicals of some of the popes on the value of working the land. I also had years of summer work on the truck farm and other farms near my growing-up home.

I decided to try to raise the money to buy the place on my own, rather than having the usual committee. People and corporations would help because they liked what we were doing, not because an important peer asked them to give.

The selling price of the property was $290,000 but we sold off that 100 acres for about $100,000, so I had to raise $190,000. We started the drive with a gift of $10,000 and ended with the same amount from the same foundation. One day I met with the owner and signed the purchase agreement on a paper bag. The owner did not like realtors or contracts, so we ended the deal over his kitchen table and that bag. I went outside and walked around some of the property, alone, singing aloud from my psalm book. It was the same version I had learned to use back in 1949, when I was sick.

Buying the farm property touched off a storm of protest. When the neighbors found out Betterway was the buyer some took to picketing the corporations and foundations we might approach for funds. They wrote letters, held meetings, and gave out press releases daily on what they would do to stop us, and the harm we would do to their peaceful community. One public meeting had 125 angry people often shouting and sometimes cursing me. Some became friends later.

They finally took us to court over our septic system being inadequate and over a zoning matter. We won these battles after two years and thousands of dollars in legal fees.

Through all this I learned to be patient, and learned that one cannot do anything about certain things, like what appears in the paper, true or not, and what people say at meetings. I again learned to take things in stride and learned that the best answer is silence, waiting out the storm.

During all the litigation, we put up a big multi-purpose addition to the house for meetings. We added a Ropes Course to the back of the property. This is an Outward Bound type course to teach leadership through physical games. We built trails and a campsite. We built a five acre lake in a valley area which has a beach and lots of fish.

It is an absolutely beautiful property. Many people use the house for retreats, reunions, meetings. The Ropes Course is also in regular use.

I do not think of the land as totally belonging to Betterway, but rather that we are guardians of it for now and have a special use of it which we share with others who are part of our life. All land really is part of the earth and "belongs" to no one. It will be gone when the world ends. We can't take it with us.

In 1988 Betterway purchased a replica of a Victorian trolley. It is like those Mary and I found in Gatlinburg, Tenn. in our trips there. Ours was made by a German-Amish company in Boyertown, Pa., over by Philadelphia. It is maroon and gold and was made for Betterway, being called the Happy Trolley of Betterway. Originally we named it the "Jolly Trolley" but another company said they copyrighted that name in Ohio and we had to change it.

The trolley is used around Elyria and the area to give tours and in parades and weddings and the like. It is good publicity for Betterway and hopefully raises funds for us. It is beautiful too, brass and wood inside, and a nice bell.

I saw the trolley as part of the fun of life, like the hot dog wagon and the popcorn wagon. These things helped people like Betterway, along with the Deli and the Search Shop. Most times when people enter a social service agency, especially if they are "sent" there they resent the place. Having such attractions helped people identify with us and our ideas. They even enjoyed bragging about being here to their friends and relatives. This is not an easy thing to achieve in the social service residential care world.

During these years new programs were added at Betterway and some old ones were dropped.

After 10 years of operating the men's Bridge Home, we closed it when the state of Ohio opened their own places and made it difficult to operate in the private sector. We added new juvenile homes until we had three group homes for boys and three for girls.

We opened our first alternative school in the former Anchor Home, closed it after three years, and opened another one, this for credit with our own teacher. In 1988 we had a hundred youth, some needing special schooling.

We had a coed group home for two years and had little more problems than the other homes, but dropped it when we needed the space for girls in that house.

All this meant a sea of people, mostly young, adrift in life, coming to us in all states of collapse, out of locked places, detox centers, drug programs, the streets and garages of their neighborhoods. Intoxicated people, mentally ill, all of these, plus retardation added to any category.

An endless stream of people, all sizes and shapes; burnt, disfigured, too fat, too skinny, missing eyes and ears and fingers. Pregnant teenagers, some already with two and three babies at age 17, and now expecting another. A third of the Betterway youth were rejected adopted kids, taken back to the adoption agency when one adopting parent died or when they got too bad in behavior.

Almost everyone was a failure in school and in "normal" society, hanging around on the fringes with the drug and alcohol and jail crowd. Afraid, with few goals, little hope for the future. Afraid of skid row down the line, afraid of marriage and the horror they had seen in family life. Most had friends or acquaintances where one parent had killed another. Most had witnessed murders and violent acts.

Almost hopeless.

Prayer

"Betterway grew like topsy. So many of my interests came into life at Betterway: a restaurant to feed people, a farm property like Grailville and the Catholic Worker and Combermere. The whimsy of the trolley and hot dog wagon and lots more kids added to the fun.

"I loved all these developments, not realizing that they took me from you Lord; they filled my heart with the cares of the world. But you had plans to settle that too."

Chapter 23

Cape Cod, Key West, Gethsemani, Prisons

Over the years Mary and I have taken trips to get away, although we stay in touch with Betterway and I usually found something relating to what I did wherever we went, relating to ideas for the store, the restaurant, the homes, the farm, the trolley, and whatever else was current.

One of the areas we return to every few years is New England: Boston, and Cape Cod. Boston is still the best people-watching place we know near the ocean, and we love to walk the shores of Cape Cod day after day. People-watching always makes me think of God, who set into being such a variety of humans, not a one of them alike, each fascinating.

We stay at the Cove Motel in Orleans, a small place sitting on a usually quiet cove (where I got the name for one of our group homes). Orleans is a few miles from a great Cape beach on the ocean, Nauset Beach, which stretches for miles. Thoreau walked and wrote along here, and Beston lived here for a year, writing The Outermost House.

When we first started going to the Cape we walked to Beston's little shack, by then the property of the Audubon Society, but it was swept out to sea in a big storm a few years ago. Beston lived there alone a year, writing a classic on the summer and winter ocean roaring up to his doorstep, the birds

Nauset Beach at near high tide in the late fall on Cape Cod. Mary and I walked this beach many times and it is one of our favorite places on this earth.

of the seasons, the smallness of man in the face of the Lord and the sea.

I have watched those same waters crash against the cliffs and sands of Cape Cod during a big storm, and, at another time, lap easily over a lip of sand at ebb tide, that moment every day when the tide reverses itself, the whole waters of the ocean pausing from their movement away from the Cape to their movement toward the Cape.

If I were to be buried at sea, I would be buried off the Cape.

We spend a few days driving to the small towns in the area, and a day at Provincetown on the tip end of Cape Cod. It is packed with Portuguese fishermen and a mix of tourists and those who cater to them, with a sizeable gay and lesbian population adding variety to the scene, and running some of the gift and art shops.

In the sand dunes and ocean grass at Cape Cod; the house is Beston's Outermost House. It was a favorite hike for Mary and me until it was swept out to sea in a great storm in 1975.

In the winter many of these same people migrate to Key West, an area of this country similar in atmosphere to Cape Cod. There is a feeling of carefreeness, joy of life, an acceptance of people as they are. Black and white couples are common, young and old, backpackers making their way around the world, people speaking different languages, (and no English), flamboyant, colorful clothing, expressions of individualism.

Some people like Provincetown and Key West so much that they stay and open a business, never having to return to the world of suits and make-believe, dresses and makeup. We go to the Cape in the fall, to catch the beginning of the winter sea.

On the years we do not go to Cape Cod we go to Key West, usually in the spring.

In Key West, an island connected to land by bridges, there is plenty of water, but no roaring surf, since reefs out in the

Atlantic and in the Gulf of Mexico break up the waves away from land, miles out. The water at the Cape is never warm, and in the Keys it is always warm, clear blue except in storms, inviting to people and creatures of the sea.

We love to walk the streets of Key West, the old part of town, with its Cuban population, a mix of black and Indian, mostly speaking Spanish or broken English. I like to walk around the cemetery, with the markers and big stones above ground to be above the water level; people are buried in these tombs, above the ground. The town cemetery is a field of faded plastic flowers, part of the bright Cuban ways.

While Provincetown and the Cape have some Catholics, especially the Portuguese, Key West's Cuban people are mostly all Catholic, with some Pentecostals and Baptists. We walk to an old, clean blue and white high ceilinged church, Our Lady Star of the Sea. Except on the hottest days the wooden louvered doors are wide open along both walls, letting in the morning breezes from the sea. The parish is served by Spanish speaking Irish missionaries from Ireland, come to help the people of the States years ago, and still here, brogue and all.

The bars in town, open all night, have heavy rock music, or Cuban-Calypso Spanish sounds. In the restaurants I have "cafe con leche" again, which I learned to enjoy with the Puerto Rican people in Lorain.

Mary has a brother and two sisters living in the southern part of Florida and we always make stops for a few days with them to catch up on family news and to enjoy their company. This includes hours of nonstop talking.

During the years at Betterway we have taken other smaller trips, sometimes to conferences in Washington, or the gift shows in Chicago, wandering around our old haunts in these cities.

Once in a while we travel down to Gethsemani, to the Trappist Monastery, made famous by Thomas Merton, the monk writer, but important to me before he was known. From my high school days, I have been going there to visit. On my first trip, about age 19, the brother at the gate let me in and asked if I had come to stay. My parents drove off for their motel. I was quick to say no, but in some ways I did stay.

My parents dropped me off at the entrance to the Trappist Monastery of Gethsemani in Kentucky. The sign above the door reads: Peace to those entering.

Gethsemani is the original Trappist monastery in this country, being settled from Europe. New Trappist monasteries spread from Gethsemani across the United States. It is a big, sprawling place, a farm, a mystical looking tall clean pure white church, filled seven times during the day and night with the chanting of the hundred or so monks, mostly Gregorian chant, as they pray the liturgy of the psalms and sing the Mass.

Lay people, men and women, attend the services or just come to pray, sitting in the balcony high in the back of the church, but during Holy Week the services of Holy Thursday, Good Friday, and the Easter Vigil are open to visitors who join the monks in the main body of the church. Mary and I did that a few years ago and I felt so at home. A part of me is always there, and during the time of my trial one of the monks wrote to me as often as he could, getting others at Gethsemani to pray. He was a regular reader of our Betterway newspaper.

After Merton started writing I read his first book, The

A recent photo of the main church at Gethsemani. For years I have felt close to this monastery. One man, Brother Thaddeus, on the right, became friends from reading our Betterway newspaper. He wrote and prayed during my trial time.

Seven Story Mountain, and the many books since then, including some being published now after his death. We carry all of his books at our Search Shop, and we sell the tapes of his classes to the novices at Gethsemani.

I have visited other monasteries especially in the East, and an Anglican one in Three Rivers Michigan and one in Cambridge, near Harvard, but my heart is at Gethsemani in the hills of Kentucky, when it comes to such places.

Prisons are also a favorite visiting place. I have spent many hours of my life in juvenile facilities, talking with kids in glass rooms, in lockup, in hallways, over coffee and pop. And hours on the outside of cell bars, feeling the humiliation of the smell of too many men in a small area, the lack of deodorant, the disinfectant on the floor, the baggy jump suits or baggy pants and shirts, the indignity of life. But beneath this all, one can find the noble spirit in most everyone.

And women too, looking even more unkempt, because women are supposed to dress up, to smell pretty. Here beauty can be found also.

One day my friend Father Connors, from the seminary summer in Sugar Grove, took me into the big prison where he was chaplain in Lucasville, Ohio, to spend time with him walking around, talking, seeing, meeting men, guards, officials, eating the prison food.

A trail of blood ran through the immense dining room area, and I was told it happened sometimes. I met the only Jewish prisoner of the more than 2,000 men. He was proud of being that one person.

In the afternoon Father Connors took me into a room saying I would be surprised in there. I was. About fifty men, all black, with shaved heads and wearing white robes, were chanting a foreign language, one or more holding up a book, the Koran. We watched a few minutes. They were facing East, eyes shut, in peace it seemed to me.

What a contrast with the blood of the dining room and the looks I saw in the "day room" where men were watching TV, and the "yard" where hundreds of men lounged around.

But here were monks. In Lucasville. Looking just like the

monks of Gethsemani. Just a cell block away from death row and the electric chair.

Years later, when I wrote up my Monasteries idea in my year of trial, a French priest who lives on Rikers Island, the prison for New York City, told me he often visited the Trappist Monastery at Spencer, Mass., and the monks reminded him of the prisoners, and the prisoners reminded him of the monks.

This scene of black Muslims at Lucasville was one of the strong sights of my life, like the man on the curb in Chicago, the dying man in the "county home." It was the inspiration for The Monasteries, the idea I like best of those I have had over the years.

Prayer

"Lord, my life continued on, the pleasures of Cape Cod, the ocean, and Key West. Every once in a while you called me back to Gethsemani. You surprised me with the sight of the Muslim men at prayer in the Lucasville prison. You used this brief scene to plant an idea in my head, The Monasteries.

"How little we realize the significance of the moment here and there in our life travels. It is one of the surprises you have for us."

Chapter 24

Cemeteries and Death

"At the going down of the sun and in the morning we shall remember them."

I found these words on a monument at the entrance to the Jewish cemetery for Lorain, Ohio.

Cemeteries are fascinating places for me. I also like to think about death.

Cemeteries in a town give me a sense of the people who lived there and they provide a meditation on the fact that we all die someday. The hundreds of people in cemeteries were once alive and involved in the same kinds of things we are, buying, selling, eating, sleeping, worrying, arguing, reading, playing, loving, and all that fills our days.

A favorite cemetery for me near Elyria is the one behind St. Martin of Tours church, this side of Valley City, Ohio, about 10 miles away. The church was put up by Germans who settled there and is a classic little Gothic structure. The date for the church was 1861, the time of the Civil War, and the cemetery came shortly after.

Clara Neff has an iron marker showing she was born in 1787 and died in 1870. Her husband Martin, 1786 to 1869, almost from the Revolutionary War to the Civil War.

One double stone marks the grave of two sisters who died at

the same time. Their two markers are joined together by a stone across the top.

In Elyria there is an old cemetery at the corner of Cleveland Street and Gulf Road, near downtown. Hundreds of cars go by every day, people going to school, the mall, the freeway, but the grounds are so quiet and rarely do people in the cars look over at the tombs. I stood and watched for this. No one looked.

Here we find the burial place of the Ely people who founded Elyria, and many old local names, Beebe, Tattersall, Boddy.

The marker for the Housman husband and wife has two stone trees with limbs touching in an embrace. A separate stone had the name, then 1858 to 1915, and "Until the Daybreak."

I also go out to the Elyria Jewish cemetery which has more familiar names. Hyman, Kaplan, Zagrans, Becker and even some stones with my family name, Peters. The first names were often biblical: Abraham, Sam, Jacob, Esther, Ben and Ruth. There was a Yetta, a name I like.

My one year of Hebrew did not help in reading the other sayings on the stones.

I found the tomb of Goldie and Morris Mayer in the Lorain Jewish cemetery. They had the Ace Hardware on Vine Avenue in South Lorain; they were a big part of my life as a young social worker there, and they helped hundreds, and knew everybody's problems. Social workers without degrees. Every city and village in the world has them.

It was almost like Goldie and her husband were alive again as I thought of all the times we talked, how they looked, how the store looked and all the people who went there for so many things, including talk.

That is the great thing cemeteries can do. The living and the dead come together again to celebrate each other.

I like some burial grounds because of their location. Down by Ashland, Ohio, is the little town of Hayesville with its cemetery south of town on a curve in the road, overlooking the beautiful hills and farmlands in the distance.

Another with a wonderful view, is in Marblehead, Mass., on a steep rocky hill above the town, looking out to the Atlantic

Ocean. The natural gray rocks mix with the tombstones, and the view of the sea is perfect for these people who made their living fishing.

For history I like the one in New Haven, Conn. at Yale University, where I found the tomb of Daniel Webster and many famous Americans.

The biggest cemeteries I have seen are for New York City. They seem to go for miles, staggering the senses.

Each of those almost uncountable markers designates an individual person who lived some time on this earth, like we do now. The little stones are often babies, the bigger ones wealthy people. Even in death the rich dwell in bigger places, as in life.

And then what: many religious beliefs hold that our bodies will rise out of the tomb, out of all those cemeteries I have been describing.

Many cultures, including our own, place objects especially loved by the dead person in their coffin or tomb. And we may dress them in their favorite clothes, and leave the reading glasses on. All of this implies that something more happens to that body.

In the Old Testament, Isaiah says, "Your dead will come to life, their corpses will rise; awake, exult, all you who lie in dust . . . the land of ghosts will give birth." And Daniel: "Those who lie sleeping in the dust of the earth will awake, some to everlasting life, some to shame and everlasting disgrace." And Jesus said, "The hour is coming when the dead will leave their graves at the sound of his voice; those who did good will rise again to life, those who did evil, to condemnation."

If our body is resurrected, which one will it be: When we were young? Or in the prime of life, or old age as when we died? What about babies who never grew up?

I believe, from reading and thinking, that our bodies will rise from the dead and we will become our whole self again, body and spirit, or soul. I will be me, Tom Peters. You will be you. But not limited by the constraints of time or years, of ages.

I will be the whole me, from birth to death, and somehow all of my bodily ages will show as one, and I will be seen with all that makes me, me. My favorite clothes, my little garden, the house plants I tended, a dog I loved, the books that mean so much to me, the people I love. My resurrected life will be all that makes me, me. And the same for you. You will be all that makes you, you.

I used to worry about Mary and I in the afterlife. She had a first husband, Brad, who died before I knew her. He was her loving husband and they had our three children. Would I be jealous? Would he be jealous? Who would be loved more? I thought about the story Jesus told about not having husbands or wives in the next life, and decided this would not be a question. We will all enjoy and love one another, rejoicing that we shared some of the same things in this life.

But before cemeteries and the afterlife, comes death.

In 1989 I was visiting my mother at the Elyria Methodist Home and several other people in nursing homes and the hospital, where dying is a routine event.

"Routine" and "dying" don't sound right together. How can something be routine which only happens once in a lifetime? It's like being born. It really is a big event.

Dying is routine for life in hospitals and nursing homes, but absolutely unique for each individual. For them it is so momentous, so awesome, gigantic, overwhelming. It is the final great act of their entire life. Nothing they have ever done before is so big.

It is not routine. We just get used to it. I imagine killing Jews became routine for the Nazis after so many thousands and then millions, but for each individual killed it was totally special.

We make such things routine because they are hard to deal with. Most do not like to think of their own death, or of getting old and feeble. I hear healthy people visiting relatives in nursing homes telling others not to let them get "that way," to let them die if they get "that bad."

On the surface, the suffering in a nursing home or hospital is hard to take. We give people sleeping pills so they, and we, will not suffer so much. But still people call out in cries for help, sometimes for hours. People moan. People groan. They ask why God does not take them. They want to die.

At these stages the relatives want them to die, too. Some find it very hard to visit when the person is so sick, or so strange in the mind that they do not talk sense as we know it. We do not understand them. Alzheimer's, we say. But even though this condition has a name now, it is no more tolerable.

Why do such people linger on? They who are so sick are like babies. I walked around the second floor at Elyria Methodist and tried to understand. Some are so thin, sitting curled up in a wheelchair or lying curled in bed. Like in the womb. If they see me, they smile with their eyes, and sometimes their faces. Some manage a small wave with just the fingers. When stroked, some blink or move slightly to show they know.

Some have medical umbilical cords, plastic tubes which bring them food and air and another to take the waste out. The womb is a room.

They are like babies, but they are not. I call them babes, which Webster's says means "an innocent person."

But why do they live on this way? I think for two reasons. One, so we can love them, care for them, visit, caress, feed and help them when it comes time to die. Like the poor or very handicapped and others who suffer, they live to enable us to be noble, to save our own souls, to please God. They live to help us live a better life so we do not die like the scriptural rich man, and go into everlasting fire.

Secondly, they live on to become purified, to get ready to see God face-to-face. When I was 19 I had that lung collapse and thought I was dying. I was in an oxygen tent (the days before tubes) for two weeks. Nothing except dying was important to me, not exams, not the food, not my family. Nothing. I was going to leave all that. I didn't even care that the nurse had to wipe me. I cared about how I would die. Period.

One way or another we get ready for death. We get rid of greed, envy, jealousy, hatreds, desires for all those advertised products, selfishness, pride, anger, self-pity, feelings of revenge.

These are often called sins. They are attachments to the things of this world. In the nursing homes we see attachments gradually fading away from the lives of the people. Life gets reduced to the simplest matters—waking up, washing, eating, sleeping, a visit, a card, a flower.

Then the person gets to where these things don't even mean much. They have to be fed, picked up, wiped. Pride is gone. The focus on "myself" is gone. Then God can enter in. We are open. We are ready for that spiritual experience.

When I am in a nursing home or place like that, I look at the beautiful childlike faces of the men and women, the quiet resignation in many, really a peaceful joy. I don't worry whether they talk or make sense. They are getting ready to talk to God, and God understands. In fact, many are already talking to God all day long. As material desires fade, spiritual enter in.

When the time of death comes we should try to be there to catch a glimpse of the joy they are experiencing, to share a little bit in that most wonderful moment when the purging ends and they are with God forever and ever. Life on earth has ended.

If we are present at such a moment, we will get a little look at what is ahead for us someday.

Prayer

"Death and the next life, or life after death. Lord, I am in awe of the possibilities. I love to visit cemeteries to help me in thinking about this. I love to attend wakes and funerals. I love to be with people at the end of their life. I am overwhelmed when I think of the wonders ahead, the moment of my death.

"At times I am fearful. It causes me to catch my breath. But I know you care for me and want me to be with you forever, so I must place my trust in you to lead me to you. At the same time I know I must do all I can to help myself. And to help others.

"Lord, bring me to you someday."

Chapter 25

Communion with the Dead

For me the dead are not dead, but living in a different world, still themselves in every way.

In my Catholic belief there is the communion of saints; we communicate with the dead. They are part of our life.

I think all of us experience this with certain people, some more than others. When a very close friend or relative dies and we view him or her in the coffin, or see a picture, or just think about them and remember their lives, we know that they are not simply gone, evaporated, obliterated. We may find ourselves talking to them, asking them to help us with some problem in life, or thinking how they would handle it if they were here. In doing this, they are here with us in some manner.

I have a special sense of closeness to those called by my church "saints" and I like to have pictures or statues of them around for my devotions. These do not become graven images or superstitious gimmicks for me any more than the statue of Lincoln in Washington is such. When I look at that statue I think of Lincoln, of all that he stood for, and I even pray that his words inspire me as I read them on the walls and look at his face with its calm strength. The Vietnam Wall memorial does the same thing for me and I had strong feelings in that war with Tom spending a year on the front lines, Mary and I not knowing from hour to hour if he was dead or alive. I get a lump in the throat and tears in the eyes looking at that image of names of the Vietnam dead.

So it is with saints, those people thought to be good examples to the living who have our respect, our attention, our imitation. Like Lincoln.

In the world of saints the mother of Jesus, Mary, is special, and I do not think of her like the others; her meaning came strongest to me in the year of trial, so I will talk about that later.

The first ordinary deceased person to inspire me was that French priest, the Cure de Ars, John Vianney. I liked and admired him because he gave as much of himself to the people who came to him as he humanly could, listening to their problems day and night, with little time to eat or sleep. The more who came to him, the more yet who heard of him from friends. I have tried to give of myself, but it is not easy at times, so I think of this small thin priest and where he is now. Rewarded.

Mostly we learn about such people by books of those who have studied them, or books they have written.

Another favorite person was St. Therese of Lisieux, France. She had become a Carmelite nun at age 15, the same community as those sisters in Columbus near my seminary. At 23 she died, but in between lived a simple life with Jesus as an intimate friend hour after hour, writing her thoughts down in a diary which millions have read for inspiration. Her picture is on the wall of my office at home where I am typing. I loved her quiet life. She died of TB, the same illness I had.

There is a story handed down in our family about St. Therese. My great uncle Sam Wimmers, an alcoholic, was very sick and perhaps dying. Relatives were praying to St. Therese for him. One day he described a nun visiting him and asked who she was. They showed him a picture of St. Therese and he said it was her. He recovered and reformed his life.

St. Teresa of Avila (no relation to St Therese) and St. John of the Cross were Spanish people who wrote in a flowery way about their inner spiritual lives about the same time in history, and knew one another. They were reformers, trying to get people back to God, and they are now called mystics. Their relationship with God was so intimate that they were carried away in poems of love, of closeness. Their lives were like the verses of the Song of Songs in the old testament. I often read St. Teresa or St. John of the Cross, a few pages at a time.

This is the reading from St. John of the Cross I love the most:

> May we attain to seeing ourselves in Thy beauty in life eternal: that is, that I may be so transformed in Thy beauty that, being alike in beauty, we may both see ourselves in Thy beauty, since I shall have Thy own beauty; so that when one of us looks at the other, each may see in the other his beauty, the beauty of both being Thy beauty alone, and I being absorbed in Thy beauty; and thus I shall see Thee in Thy beauty and Thou wilt see me in Thy beauty; and I shall see myself in Thee in Thy beauty; and Thou wilt see Thyself in me in Thy beauty; so that thus I may be like to Thee in Thy beauty and Thou mayest be like to me in Thy beauty, and my beauty may be Thy beauty, and Thy beauty my beauty; and thus I shall be Thou in Thy beauty and Thou will be I in Thy beauty, because Thy beauty itself will be my beauty, and thus we shall each see the other in Thy beauty.

This is the adoption of the sons of God, who will truly say to God that which the Son Himself said through Saint John to the Eternal Father: "All My things are thine, and Thy things are Mine."

Father Damien, the priest who went to the South Sea islands to care for lepers, is another favorite. He was Dutch. For years he addressed them in his sermons as "Dear Brethren" and then one day he started out, "Fellow lepers." He had become one of them. His story took on special meaning for me in my trial.

I admired Charles de Foucauld, who founded the Little Brothers of Jesus in the Sahara desert, with small groups of three to five people living in poverty and working with the poor. He started his community in the Sahara in 1936 and his small groups have spread around the world, including the poorest parts of New York City.

St. Augustine, from the early years of the church, the year 400, is part of my life. I read his Confessions, the story of his conversion many times, and his commentaries on life in the early church.

Martin de Porres, the illegitimate son of a white Spanish aristocrat and a black servant, inspired me to choose him as the patron or model for the Catholic Interracial Council when I helped start this organization in our area. He served food and clothing to hundreds of poor people who looked down on him because of his mixed-race parents.

Mother Cabrini, an Italian immigrant and a nun, started hospitals to help her fellow Italians and worked tirelessly to make the lives of immigrants in this country better. I hope she still watches over Cabrini Green, one of those fearsome housing projects, in Chicago.

Dorothy Day and Catherine de Hueck are seen as saints by many, including myself. Thomas Merton is similar, the Trappist monk.

St. Thomas Aquinas, philosopher and writer, is in a special category. I do not feel that I know his life, but rather his thinking. He was a big, hulking man, called the Dumb Ox, who wrote about philosophy and theology, using Aristotle as a basis, in many books which are still studied as the best thought in print on his subjects. It is deep, but when I understand an idea, it is so wonderful.

Benedict Joseph Labre is another "friend." He wanted to be a monk in a strict monastery of some kind but became nervous and exhausted after he would stay in one for awhile, so he wandered Europe as a nomad. Today we would call him a bum or a street person, sleeping here and there, visiting the great shrines of the world, but having a close connection to God, mystical, like Therese, or Teresa, or John of the Cross. He paid no attention to bathing or eating, taking scraps from garbage he would find. His worn out body was found covered with bugs and after his death the people he knew, hundreds, began to talk about his great knowledge and experience with God as he had shared it with many. A painting done of him when he was alive hangs in my office. He posed for a street artist in Italy. It is so serene and dignified, like the faces of so many street people and suffering people.

The feasts of these saints are marked by days throughout the liturgical year, and each one, day after day, seems special and enjoyable. Often the feast is on the day the person was born or died.

I also like St. Thomas, the Apostle of Jesus, who was the doubting one. Life has a lot of doubts. And St. Stephen, the first martyr, who was stoned for his faith with St. Paul looking on. And St. Paul, first a killer of Christians, then brilliant preacher and writer and traveler. St. John and his brother James, early Apostles and close friends of Jesus. St. Ignatius of Loyola in Spain, founder of the Jesuits, who partly educated me. St. Benedict and his sister, Scholastica, early monastic leaders. I have read various versions of the Rule of St. Benedict and based some of the ideas in the Monasteries on them. He was a great organizer of small groups living together.

St. Joseph is another in a special category. The foster father of Jesus, a man who had to know Jesus better than any other man in the world, the model for Christ's growing up. St. Stanislaus, from Cracow, Poland, murdered by the king when offering Mass. St. Philip a priest in Rome born in 1515 and a happy man who joked and like to make others laugh. He gathered 20 priests around him and formed a community to work and live together.

Aloysius Gonzaga, Italian, a Jesuit at 16, died at age 23 from the plague, after caring for plague stricken people for some years. He would have worked with AIDS people today.

St. John the Baptist, also special, the cousin of Jesus, a near hermit living and praying in the desert, beheaded by a king who wanted to please a dancing girl. The king and the girl are forgotten, John is famous forever. St. Peter, Paul's friend, one of the founders of the church, in a special class too.

St. Vincent de Paul, really a social worker, in France. Mary Magdalene, a favorite woman and penitent, with Jesus appearing to her before anyone else after his resurrection from the dead. Why her? She was a sinner, but she loved him.

Sts. Anne and Joachim, the parents of Mary. Saints like, Simon, Jude, and the early followers of Jesus. And St. Francis: born rich, gave away his worldly goods, lived poor, fasted, prayed, loved people, died singing.

Finally some more American saints, Isaac Jogues, John de Brebeuf, and their friends, all working among the Huron and Iroquois Indians in New York State, and after various misunderstandings put to death by the Indians for their Christian beliefs.

On one of our trips along the New York Thruway we stopped at the former Indian camp where they were martyred, beside the Mohawk River. We followed the grassy path down the ravine to the area where they died. I felt like their spirits were there with us, beckoning us to visit the place where they left this world and went on to the next.

The Communion of Saints. We can't begin to imagine what lies ahead.

Prayer

"O Jesus, I continue to think about the next life. So many millions have already lived out there time here. It is like a moment. Yet it is all we have.

"Many of those people are with you now. Some may be lost. I hope not. I look forward to seeing everyone soon. I cannot believe how fast my life has gone, how fast each day goes now.

"Keep me close to those who have gone ahead. Help me to be fit to join them, with you, forever."

Chapter 26

Books

I love books. I love words, their sounds, their meaning, their root. I love to buy and own books, to spend hours in bookstores, and in libraries. I like to admire the binding, the arrangement of words on a page, and the contents.

For those who like books, their lives are partly shaped by what they read. In this chapter I will talk about the important books in my spiritual, inner life, and my life in general to some extent.

I read the Bible almost every day, working my way through the old testament, the four gospels, and the letters and other parts of the new testament. I read in all three parts each day and prefer the Jerusalem Bible translation in English. I did have one year of Hebrew in the seminary, but no Greek, so I cannot read in any original languages.

The four volumes of the *Liturgy of the Hours*, formerly called the Breviary, are part of my daily reading, praying the designated parts from morning till night. I already talked about the importance of the books on the lives of the Cure de Ars, St. John Vianney, and St. Therese, and St. Teresa and John of the Cross.

I have read a lot of books on monastic living, but my favorite lately is *Blessed Simplicity* by Raimundo Pannikar. I also like *For the Sake of the World,* by Henry and Swearer, on Buddhist and Christian monasticism. I have all of Thomas Merton's books and like some more than others.

A big book, *Enthusiasm*, by Ronald Knox, is a regular part of my reading. This English priest explores enthusiasm in religious people, from the early days of Christianity until his day, the era of Father Divine of Detroit and other born-again preachers. He ponders the question of how we can tell genuine religious inspiration from phony or psychologically disturbed religious preaching? I still read the final chapters on discerning true spiritual enthusiasm in ourselves and others once a year.

The Mysteries of Christianity by Matthias Scheeben, and his two volumes on Mary are my best "heavy" theology books. I was led to them by Father Johannes Hofinger from Notre Dame. The descriptions of the Trinity and the Eucharist in this book are so powerful.

Another heavy author with a dozen thick books on theology was Reginald Garrigou-Lagrange, perhaps outmoded now, but still meaningful to me when I can spend the time to understand him.

Jacques Maritain was my favorite contemporary philosopher, A French-American, and I read all of his books in English and did a long paper on him. His best book for me was *Creative Intuition in Art and Poetry*, hard to understand, but full of insight on the spiritual meaning of art.

Emily Dickinson is my favorite poet. I also like Paul Lawrence Dunbar, an American black man, a real soul poet, along with Langston Hughes. I am not a big poetry reader, and it has to be simple with easy to grasp meaning. I do not like mysterious wordings in poetry, but can enjoy a little mystery and symbolism. On the humorous side I like *Cautionary Verses* by Belloc, but these are not religious.

One of the more important early books I read was *The Intellectual Life* by Father Sertillanges, which was a practical guide to organizing the days and weeks to find time to study and read. I still return to it.

I own and have read most of the series in English called *The Fathers of The Church*. These forty-some volumes contain the early writings in Christianity, after the gospels to St. Augustine, the first 300 years of my church. I wanted to know as much as I could about those times to see if the Catholic Church of today is essentially the same as it was then. Doctrines have been expanded and new thinking has come through the centuries, but for me it is essentially the same.

Theology and Sanity by Frank Sheed was a popular easy reader on this not-so-easy subject, and I was an early supporter of all the books published by Frank Sheed and his wife Masie, in their Sheed and Ward Company. They were street preachers in Hyde Park in London and we got a special thrill visiting those preachers when we were there, still arguing with the crowds, some heckling, some learning. The Sheed and Ward Publishing name has recently been started up again by the *National Catholic Reporter* after some years of inactivity, publishing old classics and new books. I like to read bits and pieces in the *Summa Theologica* of St. Thomas Aquinas.

Giuseppe Ricciotti's *Life of Christ* and his two volumes on St. Paul, along with Ferdinand Prat's *Life of Christ*, gave me a good history of those times in culture and everyday living. I relished the two volumes of *The Primitive Church* by Lebreton and Zeiller. I did a thesis on the early liturgy of the Christian church, reading every book on the subject I could find, the favorites being the *Paschal Mystery* by Louis Bouyer and *The Shape of the Liturgy* by Dom Gregory Dix, an Anglican monk. I wanted to understand everything I could about how the early Christian Mass came to evolve from the Jewish temple and personal prayers.

There have also been a lot of books about Israel, including a history by the same Ricciotti as above, and books on the ancient near Eastern texts, stories related to the old testament writings, books being written at the same time in the same styles. These texts helped me understand the creation part of Genesis, Adam and Eve and the apple, and other symbolic stories similar to writings of their times in pagan literature.

I like the long sentenced and long paragraphed readings of Cardinal Henry Newman, the English university intellectual, but I can only read him in small doses. C. S. Lewis's, *The Screwtape Letters* is a classic, along with his book on grief written after his wife died.

Studs Terkel, with *Working* and similar books gives me added insight into human everyday life. I like books on Russian icons, and any on the architecture of churches. Icons are my favorite religious art.

The Hound of Heaven by Francis Thompson has been a special little booklet all my adult life, but took on new meaning in my year of crisis.

I have read all the paperback books by the English publishers, Penguin Books, on biblical archeology, and still like to browse in them.

Little spiritual gems for me are *Introduction to a Devout Life* by St. Francis De Sales, and *The Imitation of Christ*, Thomas A. Kempis, and the more recent, *My Other Self* by Clarence Enzler, and the poetic meditations on poverty by Michael Quoist, *Prayers*.

On Death and Dying and related books by Elizabeth Kuebler-Ross have been texts I use in college teaching on death.

Other books are also part of my readings, but not the spiritual part, if we can separate that. I like books on words, cliches, synonyms, quotations, and dictionaries, the 2,500 page *Random House Unabridged Second Edition* being closest to me.

I like books of art, and favor the delicate Japanese works, and the writings of Lafcadio Hearn, who lived his life in Japan. I love the long, descriptive sentences of Charles Dickens, my favorite being *Pickwick Papers*, and in there my most-read chapter is on the elections in Eatonsville (Chapter XIII). I read this every election day.

The Little Prince is one of my favored short stories, by Antoine Saint-Exupery. It really is a spiritual book, but looks like a child's book. I like Robert Benchley for humor, and the funniest story for me is *Pigs is Pigs*, by Ellis Parker Butler, the next being *The Ransom of Red Chief*, by O. Henry, and anything by James Thurber. Most scary: *The Monkey's Paw*, and *The Rats in the Wall* in the book *Great Tales of Terror and the Supernatural*. I like everything by Langston Hughes and *Beloved*, by Toni Morrison.

Childrens: *Pecos Bill*, any pop-up books, *Where the Wild*

Things Are, and *Misty of Chincoteague*, because we go there on our trips east and look at the wild ponies and that fire station.

Classics: Chaucer's *Canterbury Tales*, Shakespeare. Oddball favorite: *Stinking Creek, the Portrait of a Small Mountain Community in Appalachia* by John Fetterman (Dutton).

For flowing words: Dylan Thomas, especially a *Child's Christmas in Wales*, which I like to read aloud. Buckminster Fuller is fascinating, and became moreso after we sat next to him, eating alone, in Marietta, Ohio, for a lecture at the college. I could hardly believe we were talking with him, and felt bad when I had to say we were going home that day, missing his talk. We should have stayed.

I could go on, but will end this chapter with a poem from Emily Dickinson:

> He ate and drank the precious words,
> His spirit grew robust;
> He knew no more that he was poor,
> Nor that his frame was dust.
> He danced along the dingy days,
> And this bequest of wings
> Was but a book. What liberty
> A loosened spirit brings!

Prayer

"Lord, thank you for books. And for the interest I have in reading books. Thank you for those who have written them and printed them. Books are another revelation of the beauty in people. We meet others through the printed word. We even come to love them, and we miss their companionship when a good book is done.

"This is another wonderful surprise in our nature, that we can communicate with others over the centuries without saying a word."

Chapter 27

In the Public Eye

My name has been in the public eye since my elementary school days. I wrote that short story about our overweight school bus driver and he put me off the bus until he cooled down. From those beginnings I was also upsetting people.

Next came four years of writing in my high school paper, finally as editor, where I was needling the administration for the way they ran things.

At the University of Dayton I wrote sports and did not cause any stir. When I entered the seminary, I began to write a column on the liturgy and family life for the *Cleveland Universe Bulletin*, the newspaper of my diocese. This continued for several years. The column was accompanied by a picture of me in clerical collar, like a priest.

Then came a lull until I entered the social work world. After I got my feet wet, I began to write about the conditions in a Black/Hispanic slum, which the community ignored, an area called "Campito," the little field.

My nose for news brought in the Cleveland papers with a full page photo story of that slum. Then there were stories on our VISTA workers. I did not write most of these, but did get the newspapers interested.

A *Life Magazine* photographer followed me around for a week, and I am in two photos in the United States book of the *Life World Library*.

Cleveland television and local newspapers did many articles on my work with youth gangs and I also wrote some articles, including a year long series in a weekly newspaper. The series was called "David" and was the story of a boy from birth into delinquency into a state institution. This stirred a lot of controversy and anger from the state. Authorities threatened to close down Betterway by taking away our license if I did not stop criticizing the state institutions. I was merely describing life as it was for all boys and girls in those places, but no one knew until then. Within the coming years the big, brutalizing guards were replaced by more sensitive people and the whole scene changed.

As the media exposure came, I got requests to give talks and seminars. Sometimes they were on the liturgy, or on race relations, but mostly they were on juvenile delinquency.

I appeared in front of school groups of students, P.T.A.s, and before many church groups. I began to take the youth gangs with me when I talked and involved them in questions and answers. In Lorain we put on a week-long series of plays on delinquency. The result was an investigation by the police over my statements about the existence of prostitution.

Sometimes I took boys and girls on TV with me to describe their lives. I took a gang to address a seminar of 250 policemen at Toledo University.

Black boys and girls were formed into speaking teams to address white audiences. We called this program "Race at the Roundtable," and presented it while youth were rioting in other cities. Sometimes the audiences were hostile, but things never got out of hand.

When the Cursillo entered my life I was giving religious talks constantly, and teaching others to do the same.

For the 20 years from 1969 to 1989 I wrote a weekly column in the Elyria paper, on my personal life. This column was cancelled after I was indicted.

The speeches came to a halt then also. The scheduled ones were cancelled for meaningless reasons when the first article appeared in the newspaper about the police searches at Betterway. People jumped to their own conclusions.

Television channels did two half-hour documentaries about Betterway and we had short parts in other films.

I learned how to handle hostility and difficult questions, how to use humor, but I still got angry at times, and showed it. Afterward I usually regretted it.

My life also was involved in attending hundreds of meetings, big and small. Meetings on the Cursillo, race, staffs, volunteers, delinquency, usually planning what was to happen next in some organization. There were countless group meetings in all our homes for 25 years, often four a week, each lasting for hours.

This all stopped after the search of our homes, long before the indictment and trial.

Even after we opened our homes for homeless adults I was not welcome to join the local task force on housing. The local AIDS group did welcome me however.

Prayer

"O Lord, you gradually led me into the public eye. I went from a school bus story to hundreds of weekly columns to months of front page news.

"Help me use my writing ability for good. Thank you."

Chapter 28

Summing It Up

That concludes much of the spiritual aspect of my life in my years on this earth from 1929 to 1988.

To a young reader, age 59 may seem like a finished time, we are what we are going to be, but to someone 70 or 80 or 90, they know at 59 much more can happen.

As we grow older the changes in ourselves build on prior years, just as our genes and chromosomes at the start of life are built on those of our parents and their parents and on back.

I came into this world with the ways that make me, me; unique, singular, one-of-a-kind. Yet I am part of what I inherited, and what I experience.

So what was I as I finished this part of life? Fifty-nine years?

Partly a farm boy, growing up around animals, manure, storms coming across fields, plants and weeds growing together, needing constant care. Chickens and goats to feed. I still love farms, animals, hay, storms.

A liking for learning and for expressing ideas in writing and talking. Health problems, down but not out. Most of my learning taking place in the tradition of the Catholic religion, Western, but some Eastern.

I came to be fascinated by the people of skid rows, jails, mental hospitals, institutions for delinquents, detention homes, nursing homes. Places where people are in misery and need someone to talk with, just sitting alone or in a small group of similar souls. I love most of all sitting down with one person, a suffering person, and talking and listening. Perhaps this makes me feel needed, but if so, I am not conscious of this. I simply get lost in the world of the other person. Sometimes, when they are difficult, I have to see Christ in them and in myself, a communion of sorts.

Life had become fairly routine by 1988, with trips to Cape Cod or Key West, to Chicago, to meetings. New books to enjoy. Opening two new group homes, buying the trolley, a fun thing. The income at Betterway was good. The farm was doing well and getting used. Business at the Search Shop and Deli needed to pick up, but it seems like business is always that way.

We had some problems over zoning in the beginning of 1988 and they lasted all year until some restrictive laws were passed in September, 1988, but they weren't too bad. We would be able to add more group homes by just complying with the new distance requirements. By now we were somewhat used to legal hassles.

I even thought a little about what I would do in a few years. Would I retire? Mary is a little older than me and works full time at Betterway, managing the office. Should she think of retiring someday?

My spiritual life, the subject of this book, was pretty routine by then too. I went to Mass every Sunday, but rarely in between. Too busy, too tired. I only read from the Liturgy of the Hours once in a while on vacation or some special feast day. I never prayed the rosary anymore, only some days said formal prayers in the morning or evening, although I would think of God often during the day. I went to funerals and prayed there. When two longtime Betterway staff died, I prayed a lot for them and spoke at the funeral Masses. Both were Hispanic and this took me back to that church in Lorain, Ohio.

Betterway kids and staff took up most of my interest and time, always taking someone here and there with me, having no time to just think or be alone or pray. I drove a nice car with gadgets, I had what I wanted in food, books, art.

We went to Key West in May of 1988, saw all the Florida relatives, had a good time. Summer went as always.

Then came August 8, 1988.

The Lord decided it was time for a change .

Prayer

"Well Lord, you brought me to the point where my life changed a lot. I never could have anticipated the next turn of events. I don't know if I was ready or not, but it came anyhow.

"You sent the right people into my life again to help me through it all. I had my own strengths and ways, weaknesses too. I could not have made it alone. You were there.

"If I had known what was coming I would have been like Jesus before his death in the Garden of Gethsemani. I would have been frightened and in a sweat.

"I didn't know I was ready, but I guess you did."

Part III

Into The Fiery Furnace

Chapter 29

August 8, 1988

"You led us, God into the snare;
you laid a heavy burden on our backs.
You let men ride over our heads;
We went through fire and through water
But then you brought us relief."

Psalm 66, Liturgy of the Hours,
Easter Tuesday, Office of Readings

It was just another summer day, typical for Ohio, not too humid, nice. It was August 8, 1988.

I was at work and wanted to find one of the staff at the boys home next door to our office, The Beacon, our first one. I walked over to look for him and no one was on the main floor, so I went up the stairs, arriving at the home's office.

A group of people were in there, seemingly milling around. A policeman in blue uniform stuck his head around the door and shut it on me. It was Rick Ellis, a young black man who had worked for us six years in that same group home. I hired him when he was nineteen, seeing leadership in him. Even then he really wanted to be a policeman but was too short.

Eventually the state said that was a form of discrimination and he did become a policeman on the Elyria force. He also married a girl who had been in one of our group homes during the six years he worked here. I was a father figure to him, and he was like a son, as were many of our staff.

Rick shut the door and did not acknowledge me, which was unusual as he normally gave me a big hug when he saw me.

In the background I saw another policeman, also black, unknown to me, and a woman social worker from the local Child Welfare Department, a former schoolmate, who had something like a tape recorder and was excited. There were some boys, I was not sure who.

Surprised, I went back downstairs and Dale Jones appeared, one of our longtime staff, at the time in the management end of Betterway. He had been director of the Beacon home where we were. I asked him to go upstairs and try to find out what was happening, and I returned to our office next door, thinking some police were talking to our boys about some crime or behavior. I had never seen them barge into one of our homes like that without staff. They would normally call the youth to the police station or to the door, but I did not think much of it. Dale said the police and the woman left when he walked into the room.

A little later Dale Jones came to find me, looking worried. He hesitated and then told me the two police were interviewing the boys and one boy claimed a Betterway person had sexually molested him, kissing and fondling him, and that person was me.

On August 23, the Betterway Board met and I told them what was happening. I also told a man, in person and in writing, from the state licensing agency, the people who approve our group homes. I was being investigated for sexual abuse by an Elyria policeman, one of two on the Youth Bureau. Rick Ellis was not active in this case and apparently only came along that first time to show the other policeman and the welfare worker where our Beacon group home office was located and how to walk into the house. No one at Betterway had given permission for their entry.

Labor Day weekend we went to see our son Don outside Athens, Ohio, on his 100-year-old property. It is remote, somewhat primitive, and I took along my psalm book, as I often did when we went there. We told Don what was happening and I enjoyed some reading, and we returned home to Elyria feeling a little better.

In early September of 1988 the Elyria City Council passed controversial legislation restricting the growth of group homes in the city. That same day we received a donation of 17 one-hundred dollar bills in an envelope, $1,700, with a note to use it. We had never received more than $10 in cash like that. We put the $1,700 in the bank that day. This had meaning later.

On Oct. 1, Mary and I left for Cape Cod. We walked the beaches, got lost in the endless waves, saw the immense swells of water from the tail end of a storm, and enjoyed the trip, but not like other years. We had a cloud over us.

I wanted to attend Mass every morning and we went at 8 in the new St. Joan of Arc church, just a block from our motel, The Cove. We walked over and stopped at a little family bakery on the way home every day. The people at daily Mass were friendly and made us feel at home, exchanging warm greetings at the peace sign time.

We returned to Elyria on Oct. 15, taking two days to drive home, and I was back in the office on Monday, October 17 to face some worried staff. Things were not going well.

While we were gone the detective was very busy, still only this one man. He was calling boys out of their classrooms in school and interviewing them, boys who lived in our group homes. He got one name from another, and knew some from his regular police work. He was asking the boys whether I had ever touched or hugged them, when, where and how I had done this. He recorded their answers on tape.

All of this alarmed the boys who knew and liked me, even if they would get angry with me over lots of small things day by day, things I would not let them do. Or blaming me for their being at Betterway rather than at home, even though they knew why they were not home.

The one detective was now working full-time on this investigation, and we began to get calls from people in other parts of the state that he had been to see them, former staff and boys. The detective broadened his questions. He was asking past and present staff about our use of money, our funding. The next Spring the police department was short of funds and needed $1,700 for new equipment, according to the newspaper. Perhaps short the same $1,700 we received six months earlier.

I knew hard times were ahead. On Thursday, Oct. 20, I had the first appointment with a man who became my spiritual director and friend, to help me through the coming times.

He replaced Msgr. Newton.

The man was William Cosgrove, the retired bishop of Belleville, Illinois, near St. Louis, and an assistant bishop in Cleveland before that. We knew one another there when I was at the Cleveland Foundation and he was active in social action areas, being the priest who helped start the Cleveland Catholic Community Action Commission, where I was a member and met those kindred souls.

Bishop Cosgrove had a brother in Elyria and when his health grew bad in Illinois, he moved into the rectory at St. Jude's parish, in retirement, to be near his brother's family. He has heart and other problems, is a large man with a quick, hearty laugh, an Irish voice, knows lots of Irish songs, and has strong feelings for the poor, the disadvantaged, minority people. He has a red, ruddy face, walks with a cane, stiff-like.

I knew I needed to talk with someone, and he was my choice and agreed to see me. I saw him once or twice a week unless one of us was out of town or he was in the hospital.

An attorney entered my life also. He was a former teacher, married to a Hispanic woman, and is very much a part of Sacred Heart Chapel in Lorain,where I got my start in social work and where I proposed to my wife, and learned about the Cursillo.

Jim Burge is a Republican, his father was an attorney and state representative from this county. Jim is precise, has a quick laugh, loves to read, has a lot of the same interests as I do, and many consider him among the best criminal lawyers in the county. I chose him on the advice of others.

In a long case like this a person comes to know their

attorney well, and they know the client. Friendships form. Eventually I learned to question the decisions of the attorney, and to trust them. On a few occasions in the beginning I asked the opinion of other attorneys on one direction or another, and they felt Jim was doing what they would do. After awhile I no longer checked.

The other main person in the coming year was my wife, Mary. We worried together, prayed, and talked a lot. We puzzled out how to tell our children and three grandchildren old enough to understand.

Our children, now grown, were Tom, managing the Betterway Deli and a daily part of our life, with his wife Karen, a nurse, and daughter Lindsey, then 9. Pam and her husband, Jack, and their three children, then 13, 10, and 2, Chris, Allison, and Seth. Both live near us in Elyria.

Don, Pam's twin, lives alone in that old house twelve miles outside Athens, Ohio, on a mud and gravel road, atop a hill. He calls his place Windy Ridge, and works on it when he is not setting tile in McDonald's or Holiday Inns or private homes. Athens is an Appalachian area, with a large state university in the town, which is where he went to school and stayed. It is a four hour drive from Elyria.

My parents, Pete and Katie, kept up with things in the case, but most of it escaped my mother who was 91 then; my father told her some, and took care of her at home. My brother Dave, five years younger than me, lives in Whitney Point, N.Y. above Binghamton, where he is an engineer. He and Eileen Mahoney have seven children, some in college, some at home, some working. They kept up on the case but were not so close because of the distance.

Elyria is a city of 60,000, Lorain, next door, 80,000, and the county about 260,000 people. We are 20 miles West of Cleveland, a metropolitan area of almost three million people. There are three newspapers in the area, three main TV channels, and some smaller ones and dozens of radio stations. All carried the news of my trial in varying degrees, the two local papers the most. In 15 months of the investigation and hearings each of the two local papers had 70 some articles, many front page, with a dozen photos of myself in each, some in color, front page.

Prayer

"O Lord, I was very frightened when this ordeal began and I would have asked that I be spared, but you never told us to take on more than we can handle with your help. I could see the possibilities ahead when I heard the first news of the investigation. I knew how it went in similar situations, and I knew how some people dislike Betterway."

Chapter 30

The Struggle Begins

> "We should be grateful to the Lord our God, for putting us to the test, as he did our forefathers. Recall how he dealt with Abraham, and how he tried Isaac, and all that happened to Jacob in Syrian Mesopotamia while he was tending the flocks of Laban, his mother's brother. Not for vengeance did the Lord put them in the crucible to try their hearts, nor has he done so with us. It is by way of admonition that he chastises those who are close to him."
>
> Judith, Liturgy of the Hours,
> Monday Morning Prayer

What was happening with me? Who was this newly appointed detective, whom I had never met, and would not know if I saw on the street? Why was he running around talking with boys and staff about me? Why didn't he come to see me if something was wrong? What would happen to my relationships with the kids and staff at Betterway and in other agencies if he kept on telling what I heard he was telling about me?

When I saw Bishop Cosgrove that first time I was so upset I did not talk at first but spent time crying. It is rare for me to cry with another person unless they are in tears and I cry with them.

He let me cry as much as I wanted. It seemed like everything I had put together for over 20 years was coming apart through the efforts of one person, who I didn't even know. I found myself angry with this unseen person, yet helpless because he was a policeman and doing an investigation, immune from questions.

Bishop Cosgrove saw me in a parish office twice, but from then on we met in the small sitting room in his area of the house, filled with the books and magazines he was reading at the time. He was always behind in his reading, and always reading.

That first meeting with the bishop was on a Thursday. On Saturday I met with Jim Burge, my attorney, for a long time and he began to ask me details of my life, lots of details. He had known of me through the Hispanic community and many others in Lorain. He kept naming people who knew me and I remembered them.

On Oct. 24, I drove into Cleveland for the hearing of a boy named Bobby, and accepted him back at Betterway. He had told the detective I molested him after he ran away from his group home to get drunk. This was the first of many times when I had to struggle to forgive someone who had "charged" me in this matter. I had to forgive them if I was going to help them. Bobby was grateful, but did not realize the harm he had caused me. I tried to like him. It was difficult. I felt sorry for him. His family life was terrible and he had been locked up in a state institution for stabbing someone in a fight. His father had tried to kill his mother and in the struggle she killed the father instead. His older brother was gay, and Bobby hated this. Bobby testified against me in my trial.

The next day I was to attend a planning meeting to be part of a program on alternative schools in Cleveland, and I went, knowing I might be unwelcome when the date arrived months later. I did not participate in the big event, because of the things that happened soon after this planning meeting.

A worry continued over my days, and Mary's too. I could not get away from thinking about the boys and staff who were being questioned by the policeman. If I told them not to talk with him, or to be aware of what he was doing, it might seem like I was trying to protect myself and wanting to avoid the findings.

I began to worry about the affection I had shown people at Betterway and how this would be seen. We worked with boys and girls in all kinds of crisis when they needed affection, in depressed states in a detention home, when a parent or grandparent had died and we were the ones to tell the youth, when a brother killed a brother in a drunken fight and we had to tell the one with us. When a parent killed the mother or father of a person with us. When a best friend committed suicide. When a girl learned she was pregnant. When a person was barely alive in a hospital from a drug overdose. We showed affection at all these times. We have worked with so many crisis situations when the only response was to hold the person in a hug. They are holding on at the same time.

I also have touched many youth on their faces, arms, bodies: an area of burns, a big scar, horrible acne, needle marks, missing fingers and hands. Kids are ashamed of these things and I found talking about them and touching them helps the person see them as not so bad. I was not afraid of them or the deformity. Some boys and girls have gone to extremes to hide their acne by combing their hair over their eyes, or tried to hide a missing hand in elaborate ways. I have always found it helpful for me and them to do the touching and talking.

But now I wondered how this affection and touching would be seen. I tried to think through how I had been with the people who were in our homes, especially the ones being seen by the policeman. Everyone in our homes was talking about this, staff and kids.

I wondered what those who were angry or mad at me might say just to have fun or get even. Kids we work with have a general dislike for police and sometimes want to fool them, or other times find it flattering that a policeman is actually talking to them nicely and not questioning them about a crime or misbehavior of their own.

They find it so exciting and unusual that they want to go overboard to cooperate and tell the policeman what he wants to hear to look even better. This is also kind of an insurance for their next bad act. They think the police will "owe them" one, that is, overlook something in the future because they were helpful.

I was now beginning to try to find ways to control my thoughts so that I did not dwell on this all the time. I knew from my past illnesses, and when I had ended my seminary training the two times, that I had to have other ideas to think about or I could not go about my work because of the worry.

I decided to get back to the *Liturgy of the Hours*, for a starter. This is a collection of psalms, prayers, readings from saints and church people, selections from the old and new testament, and thoughts on the particular feast being celebrated in the Catholic liturgy that day. This varies every day of the year. This is the official prayer of the church, sometimes called *The Office*, meaning a duty, since clergy are required to recite or sing these daily prayers. In monasteries the prayers are sung aloud together, in community.

It was the Jewish custom, in pre-Christian days, to gather for psalms and prayers seven times a day, and the new Christians, all former followers of Jewish customs, simply carried on the idea of praying seven times a day: however they Christianized the prayers, adding new things to the recitation of the psalms and other parts of the Old Testament.

Eventually these prayers were assigned set times in monasteries, beginning very early in the day, before sunrise or after midnight. Then there would be morning time prayers at sunrise, and shorter prayers during the day, (midmorning, noon, and midafternoon), then evening, and at bedtime, night prayers. The different prayer times were given names, usually from the Latin time of day, Matins being the predawn prayer, Lauds at dawn (from Latin for "praise" to signify praising the Lord for a new day). Then Prime, Terce, Sext, None, at the first, third, sixth, and ninth hours of the day (counting from 6 a.m.) and Vespers in the evening. Compline completed the day. In my seminary days I read and sang these prayers in Latin and still have those volumes which I use once in a while, although my Latin is rusty.

Over the centuries the Catholic church has changed some parts of these prayers, adding new ideas for feasts of new saints, or taking readings from new writers, people who grew in popularity at a time in history.

Today the *Liturgy of the Hours* is a long collection, needing four thick volumes to cover a year's time of seasons, varying each day. They really contain a history of the church and the relationship of Jews and Christians with the Lord. It is filled with the stories of the history of Israel, with Abraham, Isaac, and Jacob, the flight from Egypt, wandering in the desert, then settling into "the land of milk and honey" to the completion of the old testament in the Prophets: Isaiah, Jeremiah, through Malachi.

The *Liturgy of the Hours*, because it is so rich and varied each day, was the perfect prayer form to see me through the difficult times now underway. It takes about 45 minutes to recite all the parts each day, and I try to break it up according to the times of the day they are meant for, beginning about 8 in the morning, before I attend Mass, and ending at bed time.

The Liturgy of the Hours came back into my life just in time, because next I knew, I became a media sensation in my hometown and around the state as the investigation went public.

Prayer

"From the beginning I knew this experience was from the Lord, and I knew how the people of Israel had gone back and forth in their relationships with him, and how he had tested them with favors and hardships. But still I feared."

Chapter 31

Going Public; the First Spiritual Crisis

> "The enemy pursues my soul;
> he has crushed my life to the ground;
> he has made me dwell in darkness
> like the dead, long forgotten.
> Therefore my spirit fails;
> my heart is numb within me."
>
> Psalm 143, Liturgy of the Hours,
> Thursday Morning Prayer

On Nov. 11, Mary and I headed for our son Don's place in Athens. I had my book to recite the "hours" and looked forward to a weekend away from our worries.

That was Veterans Day, a holiday, and our office was closed, but that day was big for the police at a Betterway group home and at our office. They showed up at one of our newer homes and five or six police searched the place, possessed with a search warrant obtained by the detective. It said four nude sexual photos had been found in this group home and the policeman suspected there were more and came to search. Police swarmed over the place, breaking in a door in a food storage room in the basement when the staff person did not find the key fast enough. All the boys were home as there was no school. Great excitement!

At the same time, another group of policemen arrived to search our Betterway offices but found them closed. They apparently forgot it was a holiday. One staff person lived nearby and he was called by the group home next to the office and he came and let the police in. They too went all over the place, seeming to be disappointed that we were not open that day. They went through my desk where I have lots of photos for use in our Betterway newspaper, and photos that kids or staff gave me to keep.

After searching the offices in the whole house the police asked the staff person if there was anything in the basement and when he said no, they left, leaving a document saying they had taken nothing. They left a similar document in the group home they had searched. This meant they found no "evidence." The fact that they never bothered going into the office basement, which was a storage area with many boxes, told us the two searches might not really be to find things, but for some other reason, unknown at the time.

On Saturday the attorney on our board, who also was called and saw the office searched, telephoned me at Don's house. Our weekend break was over.

The search warrant, signed by the detective, said I took the four photos that summer of 1988, after "plying" a boy with wine in my office. The warrant said a boy testified to this. It also said a cook in the home where the photos were found testified that she had seen another photo. The warrant said that 12 boys testified to the detective that I had "kissed and fondled them and touched them on the buttocks." A judge signed permission for the two searches after seeing this testimony prepared by the detective.

I wondered if the police would search our house, since they found nothing in the other places, but they did not. The purpose had been achieved. In the trial we learned the prosecutor had told the detective not to search our house; he was able to imply to the jury that I had time to take sex photos from my office to my house.

The two local newspapers in Elyria and Lorain were tipped off about the searches and told that I was the focus, there were sex photos, 12 boys had talked. They had come forth.

A friend at the Elyria newspaper, who worked as a Betterway staff person for some years, and lives around the corner from our office, told me they would get a copy of the search warrant, and print a story the next day. He wanted my comments on what was happening. I told him I could not talk about it on the advice of my attorney. I did not tell him who this attorney was and later the papers said they had inside information on who it was and named someone else.

On Wednesday, Nov. 16, I had a speech after lunch at a women's group, meeting at the YWCA hall in Elyria, across the street from the group home that was searched.

As I walked in the hall I passed the newspaper stand, and there was an article on the front page, saying our group home and office had been searched, and I was the focus of a police investigation.

I knew that was the big day. My life would never be the same again. I gave the talk, on the topic they chose, "Betterway: 23 years later." Toward the end I spoke about the article I had seen and what this would mean. I had only seen the headlines, but I knew.

The women spoke up for me, saying I had done good over the years, that boys must be mad at me and saying those things, whatever was being said, and they would be loyal to me. There were about 50 women present.

That was my last public speech to the time of this writing. The few other talks I had scheduled were cancelled by the groups. They all had reasons for cancelling, and no one said it was related to my new situation. They said they would call on me again. None did.

That same day the neighboring Lorain paper had my photo on the front page, and a much bigger article. The next day the Elyria paper carried a large color photo on page one of the searched group home. From then on the two daily newspapers seemed to try to outdo each other in photos and boldness of story and headlines. Sex sells.

The morning after the first article, after that speech, I went to Mass at St. Jude's church and saw Bishop Cosgrove again. He mostly listened those days, and gave little phrases of

Going Public; First Crisis 173

Teens' charges lead to cop search of group home

By SCOTT STEPHENS and STEVE NOVAK
C-T Staff Writers

ELYRIA — Elyria police [...]ing to sources.

The search warrant was issued Nov. 10 by Lorain County Common Pleas Court Judge [...] Corts and was executed [...] same day.

[...] warrant sought information pertaining to alleged sexual [...] of boys under Betterway's [...]. The warrant specifically [...] nude photographs that [...] believed to have been [...] of the boys [...] group home, called The [...]

Betterway sex photos are probed

By Rick Zarbaugh and Hank Kozloski
[...] Staff Correspondent

ELYRIA — The Betterway Inc. office and one of the organization's group home were searched Friday by Elyria police for sexually explicit photos of young boys and other items, sources have told The Journal.

[...]

Tom Peters is target of sex probe

By SCOTT STEPHENS
C-T Staff Writer

ELYRIA — Thomas H. Peters, executive director of the Betterway Inc., is a target of an investigation of alleged sexual misconduct at one of the organization's group homes for delinquent youths.

TOM PETERS

[...] ency. The agency operates six [...] homes for delinquent

Grand jury gets Betterway probe

By Joanne Allen
Journal Staff Writer

ELYRIA — An investigation of alleged sexual misconduct in Betterway Inc., a group home and social service agency in Elyria operated by Thomas Pete[...], will be considered [...] Lorain County [...]

[...] of the Elyria [...] county prose[...] has been [...] plaints for [...] target of the [...] be Peters, [...] e organiza[...]

[...]ria police [...]rrant at a [...] youths, a [...] Bridge, [...] shop and [...] at the Huntington [...]

Peters indicted for sex with boys

By Joanne Allen
Journal Staff Writer

ELYRIA — Thomas Peters, the 59-year-old executive director of Betterway Inc., was indicted yesterday for sexual offenses involving young boys in the agency's group homes.

Peters, of Elyria, was served with 25-count secret indictment. He was booked on the charges at noon yesterday at the Lorain County jail and released on $7,500 bond.

The indictment, handed down by the Lorain County grand jury

Betterway indictment is issued

By Hank Kozloski
Journal Staff Writer

ELYRIA — A secret indictment was handed down yesterday by the Lorain County grand jury in the probe of alleged sexual misconduct concerning Betterway, according to a source [...]

[...] several months of investigation into the charges conducted by the Elyria Police Department's youth bureau, the source said.

Thomas H. Peters, 59, is executive di[...] [...]terway, [...] ago.

[...]et six [...]nt boys [...] years [...] as a [...]rm

Grand jury indicts Peters

C-T Staff Report

ELYRIA — Thomas H. Peters, executive director of The Betterway Inc., has been charged with 25 counts of sexual misconduct involving 11 juveniles who had lived at agency's group homes for quent boys.

The charges — one felony the rest misdemeanors contained in a secret indictment issued Tuesday by a

Charged with 25 counts of sexual misconduct

County grand jury.

The felony charge — "illegal use of a minor in nudity-oriented performance" —

a minor to engage in sexual activity) and "sexual imposition" (improper contact).

Lorain County Prosecutor Gregory White said the sexual charges involve [...] zones" [...]

dent of The Betterway Board of Trustees, announced today that Peters has requested — and been granted — a leave of absence from his job as director of the agency "pending a disposition of the charges."

[...]bert Sprague, Betterway's [...] the past 11

Reagan said the board has been aware of the investigation of Peters for several months and "has tried to respond appropriately to it, although specific information concerning the accusations has not been communicated to us.

"Betterway remains committed to its program and to its future."

While the indictment names the 11 youths, it pinpoints the

Tom Peters enters plea of innocence

By SCOTT STEPHENS
C-T Staff Writer

ELYRIA — Thomas H. Peters, director and founder of Betterway Inc. group and foster homes for troubled youth, pleaded innocent this morning to 25 charges of alleged sexual misconduct involving 11 boys in the program during the past several years.

Peters, who was indicted on the charges by a county grand jury Dec. 27, entered the plea during his arraignment before Lorain County Common Pleas Court Judge Floyd D. Harris. He was accompanied by his lawyer, James Burge.

He faces a pre-trial hearing Jan. 20 before Judge Joseph Ciriglliano.

Peters, 59, is charged with one felony, the illegal use of a minor in nudity-oriented material or performance.

The other 24 charges — 12

On B-1: Betterway counselors' credentials probed

counts of importuning and 12 counts of sexual imposition — are misdemeanors stemming from 12 alleged incidents of soliciting minors to engage in sexual activity and then having improper contact with them.

The felony charge carries a maximum penalty of 15 years in prison and a $7,500 fine. The misdemeanors are punishable by up to six months in jail and a $1,000 fine on each count.

Lorain County Prosecutor Gregory White said the sexual imposition charges involve "touching the erogenous zones" of the youths. The boys were all between the ages of 13 and 17 when the alleged incidents occurred, according to the indictment.

The charges resulted from an

PETERS (RIGHT) WITH ATTY. JAMES BURGE
C-T/Bun Chan

Elyria Police Department Youth Bureau investigation based on complaints from former and current home residents. The investigation culminated in November with a police search warrant raid of Peters' Middle Avenue office and at The Bridge

group home on West Avenue.

No photographs were found in the raid, but police had reportedly earlier obtained one sexually explicit photograph believed to be the basis for the felony charge.

wisdom and encouragement and told me to keep up the prayers of the "hours" and keep my mind busy.

That afternoon Mary and I went to see Jim Burge, my attorney, to talk about the new developments and how we would pay for what he would be doing.

By now I figured everyone who knew me in the county knew about what was being said and I had to begin to deal with all that. The impact of being seen as a public sex offender had not begun to sink into my mind. It was too overwhelming at this point.

The next week was Thanksgiving. We had all our family over for dinner, as always, but it was subdued and at the meal prayer I asked the Lord to help us in whatever was ahead. After dinner we talked about it some.

In the next days I was overwhelmed by all that was happening. I still went to our Deli restaurant to help out with the register at noon when I could, but felt funny. On Nov. 30, I went to a breakfast meeting of social workers in the county and got mixed reactions. Some people wished me well, others asked what was happening, others said nothing about my situation, perhaps not knowing yet or perhaps not knowing what to say. I could not tell.

In the next weeks I found a "wondering" in myself. Wondering what others were thinking was present the rest of the year. There was no way to tell if someone was snubbing me or just busy with their own ideas. I found myself wanting to know.

That breakfast, with about a hundred of my "peers" was my last formal attendance at anything in my home county with social workers for over a year. One man noticed I was occasionally wringing my hands while I was standing in line for breakfast and asked if I was sleeping well as he looked at the hands. He offered no words of comfort.

I walked into a neighborhood store near our group homes and the owner, working alone, looked at me in surprise and said it was really something that this was happening in a little town like Elyria. I thought he made it sound like a mass murderer had been discovered.

Then he started to tell me some of his problems. This man

had never talked with me about his life before, and I had stopped in his store for years. He only talked when he had a complaint about one of the boys or girls from our group homes. Then I was the director of Betterway. Now I was a person with problems just like himself and he could talk to me in a new way.

As time went on I noticed this subtle change in others who had been in trouble or in jail. I was one with them now.

When I went to evening Mass I got an unusual reaction from one man. I had known him for years and he worked with me at one time, but now he did not speak. At communion he began to time his participation so that he would get in line just in front of me. Several times he pushed others out of the way and once bumped into Mary to cut in front of us. I finally decided he was trying to protect the Eucharist from me. One day he just stopped coming to daily Mass and that ended. I guess he decided I was unworthy to receive Communion.

Prayer

"Lord, I was reeling from what was happening to me. I did not grasp it, but you were going to reduce me to nothing in the eyes of the public and take away my pride, my reputation, my world. I was not prepared, but that did not make any difference. No one can ever be prepared."

Chapter 32

Spiritual Developments; Mary

> "Come to me, all who yearn to be filled with my fruits,
> and you will yet hunger for more.
> For all who try me will find my memory sweet.
> Mother of holy hope and of love everlasting,
> O pray for us."
>
> Liturgy of the Hours,
Evening hymn for a feast of Mary

I was seeing Bishop Cosgrove twice a week for an hour or so and getting around to some of my 1988 Christmas work at Betterway. I send out about 250 letters each Christmas, personal notes to people who send us donations. We also put out a holiday edition of the Betterway newspaper a few weeks before Christmas. I tackled these jobs and got them done, talking in my column in our newspaper a little about what was happening to me. That was our last paper published until I returned as director the next fall. I have never found anyone else to publish the paper.

A few days after that social workers meeting, I drove into Cleveland to see some of the people where we did youth business all the time and had weekly contacts. They were cold and did not seem to want to see me and wished me luck, like a duty. The detective had talked with them, telling all the evidence he had of what I was doing. They had known me for years, but the thought of sex abuse rings a strong note. It frightens people and takes away their ability to think things through.

By then I was praying the Liturgy of the Hours every day. It was the Advent season, with thoughts of getting ready for Christmas.

I had to have a place to say these prayers and usually just stayed in church before and after Mass, and stopped in again later in the day. This was a peaceful place, a refuge. I went to St. Mary's church and to St. Jude's and to any Catholic church I could find if I was out of town.

I discovered that Sacred Heart Chapel, the Hispanic church in Lorain, had a special service every Thursday. All day long the sacrament of the Eucharist would be displayed in a gold and glass container for all to see, to inspire devotion. This is an older custom in the church called Exposition of the Blessed Sacrament. It is not done much any more, but I like it. People would come in and pray, usually for an hour.

An hour of private prayer in a Catholic church is traditional, chosen to mark the time Christ asked a few of his apostles to watch an hour outside the Garden of Gethsemani while he prayed, weeping and thinking of his coming death the next afternoon. The apostles were tired and fell asleep, and Jesus chided them for not being able to watch and pray for just one hour with him.

When Catholics pray an hour in church, like those people at Sacred Heart, it is called making a "holy hour." This came back into my life more a little later. Holy hours had been part of my novitiate and seminary days.

In those days of the investigation I could not kneel or sit in church and just meditate for an hour because of all the gloomy thoughts that would come to mind. I kept thinking, what if this happens, or that, I should say this, or that, and on it went.

I started reading the Bible more, Old Testament, Gospels, and the Acts to Revelation. Reading some in each part each day.

The rosary came back into my life. Many Catholics do not use it in the modern church, and I had not recited those prayers for some years. The rosary is a form of prayer beads used for "counting" prayers and common to many religions.

In the rosary a person recites the Apostles Creed, three "Hail Mary's" and a "Glory be" and an "Our Father" and then recites a series of 10 Hail Mary's, thinking of different religious events in the life of Christ and Mary for each 10. These events are called "mysteries." Some days of the week they are joyful, like the birth of Jesus, other days sorrowful, like the death of Christ, some days glorious, like the resurrection.

One can either concentrate the mind on the words of the Hail Mary and the other prayers, or think of the various mysteries.

The first half of the Hail Mary is from the New Testament story when the angel appeared to Mary to tell her she would be the mother of the awaited Lord. The second half of this prayer is an early one to Mary. The Glory prayer is used often in Catholic liturgy and is one of my favorite short ones: "Glory be to the Father and to the Son and to the Holy Spirit, as it was in the beginning it is now and ever shall be. Amen."

I began to enjoy reciting the rosary, but had to look up the traditional mysteries for each day, it had been so long since I recited them.

Eventually the praying of the rosary became like sailing in a small boat, alone, taking me away from my miseries. It was like Mary took me away, as I thought of the mysteries or the words, varying my attention between both.

I do not like saying the rosary in a big group unless it is recited very slowly so I can think of what I am saying. The rosary continues to have this soothing effect in my life. I sail away.

One day in my morning shower, my mind was filled with thoughts of the problems at hand and I began to recite the "Hail Mary" prayer very slowly, one word at a time. My worrisome thoughts left. I enjoyed the ideas in this prayer so much, word by word. The words took up my attention. I now use this prayer to Mary any time my worries get out of hand.

This was a part of my longtime love for words, going back years. I started using this slow "Hail Mary" prayer in bed at night, upon waking up, and any other problem time. "Hail Mary, full of grace, blessed are you among women, and blessed is the fruit of thy womb, Jesus," goes the first half of the prayer, which is about as far as I get and my head is clear. "Holy Mary, Mother of God, pray for us sinners, now and at the hour of our death, Amen," is the second half.

This use of these words was not something unconscious with me. I was aware that these words helped me and decided to study more on the theology of Mary and her role in religion. I used that book *Mysteries of Christianity* by Scheeben, and another two volume work he did, *Mariology*. These are slow going and profound.

I took to thinking a lot about Mary, and loved to think how Jesus must have felt about his mother. One day I was kneeling in church in front of the tabernacle and the Eucharist, which Catholics believe is bread changed into the body of Christ, and a thought hit me:

Jesus was completely made from Mary. In our theology he had no natural father, the Holy Spirit was the instrument conceiving Jesus in Mary, so he would be God and man. St. Joseph was his foster father. But the Holy Spirit has no body to contribute any of the genes and chromosomes to Christ's formation. Unique among all humans, Jesus comes physically totally from his mother. That means the Eucharist in front of me, which I receive in Holy Communion, the physical part of the Body of Christ, is totally from Mary.

Mary is now an immense part of my spiritual life. I do not even think about Jesus being jealous of any attention people give to his mother. I love to read about the places where Mary has appeared to people all over the world, little people: Lourdes, Fatima, Guadalupe. I love to visit the shrines and chapels and churches dedicated to Mary.

"Turn then, most gracious advocate, your eyes of mercy toward us,
and after this exile show to us the blessed fruit of your womb, Jesus.
O clement, O loving, O sweet Virgin Mary!"

Liturgy of the Hours,
from the closing hymn at night prayer.

Prayer

"O Mary, you helped me as I struggled to keep my head above the waters. I had loved you over the years, but now I needed you more than ever. And you came. I thank you for making the rosary a part of my life again."

Chapter 33

The Eucharist, the Poor Clares, and Eternity

> "Know that in this bread is the body of Christ
> which hung on the cross . . .
> take, therefore, and eat his body . . .
> and you will become members of his body.
> Eat this sacred food,
> so that your bond of unity with Christ may never be broken."
>
> Liturgy of the Hours,
> Feast of Corpus Christi, Reading Prayer

During the time that I was getting a new appreciation and devotion to Mary the mother of Jesus, I was also finding new meaning in the Eucharist, the Blessed Sacrament, the bread that has been blest at Mass and becomes, in Catholic belief, the real body of Christ. And in Christian belief, Christ is God. This sacrament is kept, looking like bread, in the tabernacles of Catholic churches across the world.

This is a difficult idea for people to accept who are not Catholics, and even Catholics never grasp the full meaning. If this is a truth, then this is God under the appearance of bread. An absolutely staggering thought, if we believe that God created the world and all that is in it, the stars, the heavens, the earth, the plants, every human being. And God sustains creation in existence. When we die God will be part of our judgment as to where we live eternally, never ending. If this is true, it is beyond the imagination. And this living bread becomes part of our body. It does not melt away. It becomes us, like our other food does.

If it is not true, if the bread is just a symbol of God, a reminder, like a statue is a reminder of someone, then it is a different matter. There would be no reason to kneel for hours in front of the Eucharist, to genuflect, to pray in that direction, to lock the tabernacle. If it is not Christ, it is a hoax, or a deception of 2,000 years.

If I go back to that Thursday Passover meal, and listen carefully to Christ, and look at what the people there thought, and the people the following years, who knew the people who were there, and the people of the centuries since, then I have faith that this is Christ, God. This presents a direct way to communicate with our maker. "This is my body" is what Jesus said when he gave out the bread to his friends. This is me, he said. A hard saying, they said. I agree, he said. But this is me, take and eat.

I took out the book of *The Mysteries of Christianity* again and read the long chapters on the Eucharist. How can this look like bread but not be bread. How can what looks like bread be God? Philosophically and theologically a lot of this can be understood. It takes careful reading and thinking, and rereading, but it can be partly understood, at least to the point of knowing for sure it is not impossible. It is possible, like a miracle can happen.

The *Summa* of St. Thomas has a lot on the Eucharist, as does the layman's explanation of the book, *The Companion to the Summa*, by Walter Farrell (Sheed and Ward). I read the gospel accounts of the last supper, over and over, and I knelt in churches in front of the tabernacle trying to grasp what I knew to be true.

I knelt in the basement chapel of St. Mary's church for hours, and at Sacred Heart Hispanic church, with the Eucharist displayed on the altar. I knelt at St. Jude's church. The side Eucharist altar is low and close.

One day coming back from Cleveland, December 16, I stopped at a little chapel off the freeway in the suburb of Rocky

River. I had remembered it from years back, in my seminary days.

It was a quiet chapel, the muffled sounds of airplanes from the nearby airport and the soft chanting of the nuns breaking the silence. The Eucharist here was kept day and night in a gold and glass container, showing the bread between golden angels. It sits high above the altar in an opening in the wall. On the other side of the wall are some nuns called The Poor Clares, a branch of the Franciscans. The Poor Clares were started to beg money for the poor and to take turns praying day and night before the Eucharist.

At different times in the day visitors can hear the singing of the Liturgy of the Hours, the chanting of words. The visitors side, where I sat, has about 15 pews, all light colored wood, highly waxed. There is a marble floor and altar and the smell of burning wax candles and incense.

Because of the open design in the wall separating the two

The Franciscan Poor Clare's chapel of perpetual adoration outside Cleveland, with cloistered nuns on the other side of the wall. The Eucharist is in the center opening above the altar, between the two chapels. A favorite stopping place for me.

chapels both groups, the visitors and the nuns, could pray before the Eucharist and see it. On my first stop I thought I might stay twenty minutes or so and then I would be thinking of my problems and have to go on. I stayed an hour, reading bits from booklets in the seats, from the New Testament.

I came many times after, often the only one there. It is so silent. Sometimes I stayed more than an hour, unable to leave. It was escape from my difficult world, into a beautiful one.

One day, kneeling in front of the Eucharist, alone, in the basement chapel at St. Mary's, I was struck by the fact that eternity was here. If I could cross over the invisible boundary between what I saw and what was, I would see God, eternity, all the saints, Mary, and the next life meant for all of us. I was kneeling in front of the planets, the stars, the moon, the sun. I did not have to go to the moon to explore. It is all here.

My troubles are nothing. The investigation, the newspapers, the looks of people, my feelings. Nothing. Here is everything. The beginning, the end. God.

I was in tears. I went up and placed my hands and arms on the tabernacle. I stood there. I knelt down. I put my head on the table holding the tabernacle. Here I was. Here is God. What else matters.

Since then these thoughts have come to me different times, including when I am not in church. God is here, right here. I wanted to keep the Eucharist in a home tabernacle, but was told it was not a good idea, so I found Christ at my home and made a place where I could pray in my office.

The Eucharist comes into the church through the Mass. But the Mass day to day in many parishes can be boring, lacking the life and participation I knew at Notre Dame, Harvard, a few other places. And the sermons are sometimes boring, whether they are short or long. Priests seem to preach lessons from books, not from the heart. Priests are much more spiritual in person, just talking, than in the pulpit, preaching. I think many are afraid to show their feelings in public pulpits.

The Mass could be so much more interesting if people stood or sat or knelt around the altar, facing one another, instead of looking at the backs of one another. The high point of the Mass for most people, when they look alive, is at the exchange of peace, when they greet one another, and when Mass is ended and they talk and visit.

Worship in the time of Christ had a lot of people-interaction, plus dancing, singing, the playing of harps, cymbals, wailing, crying out, and praying aloud. That's how the Jews prayed, and the early Christians.

Prayer

"O Jesus, I am overwhelmed by this mystery of the Eucharist. Every time I stop in church or think about it I am in wonderment. I should stay in church all the time, day and night. What can anyone do to harm me within this presence in my life?

"O sacrament most holy, O sacrament divine, all praise and all thanksgiving be every moment thine."

Chapter 34

The Bible

"Your love, O Lord, sustains me.
In the midst of all my troubles,
your consolation gladdens my soul.
As we share abundantly in Christ's suffering,
so through Christ we share abundantly in his consolation."
Liturgy of the Hours,
Sixteenth Sunday in Ordinary Time,
Office of Readings

Shortly after entering this time of trial, I had begun reading the Bible more. The Sunday liturgy at Mass does have bible readings, so there is this weekly sampling, but Sunday services have so many other parts, the singing, the people, the preaching, that the bible readings can get lost.

Once before I had read the bible all the way through from beginning to end, and had read parts a number of times, and the gospels a lot. But now I had a craving to be reading all the main parts, Old, New, Acts, and Letters and Revelations. So I started out in the beginning of all three parts, and am still doing that. I get through the whole Bible in a year.

The Liturgy of the Hours, in the predawn readings and prayers, has a lot from the Bible, often the Old Testament, with a sermon or article by some saint as a commentary on this reading.

The more I read, the more I identified with the Jewish people, the promise or covenant the Lord made to give them their own land, their weaknesses in honoring the Lord in spite of the promises, their begging forgiveness again. Coming back again.

I was struck that story after story was about the Lord's favors to Israel, their failures, their struggles, the Lord's acceptance. These were told in tales of the flight from Egypt, the crossing of the Red Sea, the pagan idols, the many rulers, kings with strengths and weaknesses. Connivings, battles, romances, family feuds, treachery, love, murder, killings, burials. All the things that we experience in our lives and world.

The story of the Jewish people and their Lord is the story of all people and their Lord, individuals and groups. We fall, we rise, we fall, we rise, we fall, we rise. God is angry with us, calls us, forgives, watches, forgives again.

Genesis is the story of the beginnings, Revelations the endings. Jeremiah and Isaiah had struggles, and Job with his "Naked I came into the world, and naked I leave it. The Lord gives and the Lord takes away. Blessed be the name of the Lord." Whatever the Lord gives, we should bless the Lord for it. I began to apply that to my situation.

I applied the whole Bible to my experiences. God gives me difficulties because he loves me. He tests me that way, just as he did the Jews. The Lord takes away our good things so we will weep and ask his help. The exiled Jews, far from home, cried out: "There by the waters of Babylon we sat and wept when we thought of you O Lord."

The very best in this kind of thinking is found in the psalms. David laments his falling away from God, he wanders in the desert, seeking. He cries out his feelings in the psalms. Day after day I find strength to live and have joy in whatever is happening by praying the psalms as I find them in the Liturgy of the Hours. They are the greatest, most emotional, most intellectual, most loving words I know in my relationship with God. The Catholic liturgy is so arranged that most of the 150 psalms are recited every four weeks, making for variety, and excitement.

These same prayers were the ones that woke me to the existence of God when I was 19 and recovering from that collapsed lung. They were my first real contact with God, and are still the best one, forty years later.

I like the book of Lamentations.

The Song of Songs has a special, mystical, place in my life, and I have more on this later.

In the New Testament, I like the gospel of St. John the most. He was closest to Jesus, a lover of people. He is the most profound in his thoughts about Jesus. I love the very most chapters 13 - 18 giving the talk of Jesus to his friends before he was arrested. I never tire of reading this, called his farewell discourse ". . . do not let your hearts be troubled . . . I am the true vine . . . if the world hates you . . . you will be weeping and wailing while the world will rejoice."

The passion and death of Christ in all four gospels are my other favorite parts.

The Acts are so interesting because they tell about the life of the people as Christianity was getting underway, replacing the Jewish religion for some people.

St. Paul was a tireless man, spending great energy going after the new Christians, then being knocked down by Christ and told to come to his senses. He did, with just as much energy, and began his preaching to promote the religion he was persecuting. He apologized to the Lord for his former behavior and said he was not worthy of these new tasks, but the Lord told him to get going on his work and paid no attention to his past.

His letters to the various churches are full of meaning, sometimes simple, sometimes complex. The Book of Revelations is glorious in its glimpses into the next life, trying to capture in words what we will experience. It too seems mystical and can be read over and over, even though we do not understand it all.

During these difficult times for me the people of the Bible became intensely real and personal. I enjoyed recalling their stories, their trials and tribulations, their wanderings, loneliness, joys, good times. Their constantly seeking God and never getting there.

The people of the Old Testament used to seem distant and

remote, like another religion. On Passover, 1989, the day I returned to work at Betterway, we celebrated the meal with Jewish friends in Elyria. It was my first Passover meal, but I felt as if I was stepping into part of my past. I felt at home with the ceremonies. They are part of my culture, my people, my inheritance.

This intimacy continues as I read the Bible today, feeling close to the Jewish people, and when I read the New Testament in church it is like sitting down with Christ to read over an adventure he had or a talk he gave or an emotional experience in his life.

It is like looking through the books and boxes of old photos which families do at holidays and special times. Looking with Jesus.

Most of all the psalms seem to fit me, my situation, my moment, right now. They have had this universal quality to fit the life experiences of millions of people over the past three thousand years or so. The creator of people had to be the same person as the spirit behind the psalms. They seem divinely inspired.

Prayer

"Oh Lord, thank you for the beauty of the scriptures. The readings sustained me in the struggles of my days of trial."

Chapter 35

"Get Out of the Way"

> "Your body is the temple of the Holy Spirit,
> who lives within you,
> whom God has given you, you are not your own any more."
> St. Paul, 1st Letter to Corinthians,
> Liturgy of the Hours, Wednesday, 22nd wk.
> Ordinary time, Readings.

In December of 1988, late in the season of Advent, I found a very thin red book in my library at home with the name *The Akathistos Hymn* in gold letters on the cover. I do not know where I got it.

I looked through it and found this was a hymn to the Theotokos, Greek for the Forth-bringer or Mother of God. It is used some in the Catholic and Orthodox Eastern Byzantine Rite the first four Saturdays of Lent and even more on the fifth Saturday of Lent, called Akathistos Saturday.

It consists of 24 stanzas, alternately shorter and longer, with each shorter one ending in "Alleluia," and longer one ending in "Hail, Bride unbrided!" Each of the longer stanzas starts with "Hail!"

It was written in the year 626 to honor Mary, the mother of Christ, who was seen as instrumental in saving the city of Constantinople, the chief city in the East, and the passageway city between the East and Europe (today the city is named

Istanbul). The city was under attack by the Persians and the citizens marched around the city all night, holding up pictures of Christ and Mary and Eastern saints, singing and praying to be saved. The ships of the Persians were destroyed in a storm that came up and the people were saved on that night. The next day they started writing the Akathistos Hymn and it has been part of the Eastern Liturgy of the Hours ever since.

It struck me as absolutely beautiful, the most wonderful thoughts and words about Mary I had ever heard. I started to read parts of it and felt beside myself with joy, realizing also that it went back so far in history.

I did not read much of it. It was too beautiful. It was a gem to put off for a special time. I decided to save it for Christmas, sometime during the day.

We went to Midnight Mass at our little church in Elyria, the other Sacred Heart, and I was distracted. The newspapers had articles saying I was going to be indicted any day now.

The next morning, Christmas, I went to the basement chapel of St. Mary's church, my childhood church, and intended to read or pray the Akathistos Hymn and then go to the upstairs church to receive Communion at the 9 a.m. Mass. I would normally attend Mass as part of receiving communion, but this was Christmas and I had been to Mass.

I was reading the hymn and asking to be given direction on what I should do with my life, now that I might be indicted and so much had changed in my work. If I got indicted we had planned that I would take the voluntary leave of absence to keep the welfare departments from taking boys and girls out of our homes.

I was looking for some kind of inspiration to leap out at me from this hymn. I was also listening to the hymns above me to know when it would be Communion time.

At the right time I slipped quietly up the back stairs which lead to the back of the main church and stood there. People were around me as it was a standing-room-only Mass because of Christmas. It was time for Communion. I was watching the front of the church and planning when to go up.

Communion started. Suddenly a man faced me and said somewhat loudly, "You're in the way." I guessed he was an usher, but I did not know what he meant. He said it more forcefully, again. Then another man joined him and said "Get out of the way." Gruffly, in some anger. I still did not know what they were talking about and then the first man put his hands on my shoulder and suddenly turned me around, saying "Do you want to go to Communion?". He was not doing it gently, and I was getting angry at these two men.

When he turned me completely around I was inches in front of a man holding out the communion wafer, saying to me "The Body of Christ." I instinctively took the bread and in embarrassment went back downstairs, flustered over this scene. I was still heated over what they said and did. I had forgotten that they served communion in the front and rear of this church when it was crowded.

I knelt down before the chapel tabernacle to catch my emotions and start reading the Akathistos Hymn again, but I was too agitated. Then I went over what they had said several times.

"Get out of the way. You're in the way. Get out of the way. Get out of the way."

That was my Christmas message, my gift from the Akathistos Hymn. I should get out of the way and let God do things with me. I was in the way of what he wanted to do. My pride, my worries over what people might think or say, my concern for my future. My need to control my life, my surroundings. I was usually in charge.

I went on with the hymn, reading it all the way through for the first time, and crying. The words were more beautiful than I imagined they would be. Each stanza builds on the prior one and leads to the next and as I write this I have now read it hundreds of times and still find new meaning each time.

I was overwhelmed all that morning, at the beauty of this prayer and the wonder of the message to me. At what had happened to me. I also had the feeling there was not much I could do except "get out of the way." It would not be in my hands. I had to abandon myself to trust in God to lead me along.

The two ushers have faded from my life. I had seen them

The chapel in St. Mary's church basement where I often go to pray. I was reading the Akathistos Hymn here on Christmas of 1988 when I had that surprise.

around St. Mary's before, faithful ushers, nicely dressed, keeping things in line, doing their job. They may have thought I had been drinking the night before or was "out of it" for some other reason. In any case, I was definitely in the way of the communion line.

The Akathistos Hymn is part of my life now. I recited it every day in the month of May, 1989, a time dedicated in my church to Mary, the Mother of God. I recite it all or in part many other days, and did so before sitting down to write this section. I translated the hymn into modern English and it was the first book published by Betterpub Press.

I will end this chapter with the opening part of the Akathistos Hymn, which celebrates the actions and words of the angel messenger coming down to Mary to tell her she is now with child, who is God.

The Angel who was bodiless, having heard the bidding secretly in his soul, went with haste to Joseph's dwelling and said to the Unwedded One:

> He who in his condescension bows the heavens down is housed unchanged and whole within you.
> I see him take the form of a servant; and wondering I cry to you:
>
> HAIL! BRIDE UNBRIDED.

Prayer

"O Lord, you surprised me that morning in church. I was looking for a great message and got a simple one, "get out of the way." Please help me to get out of your way so you can use me for your good. I do not know what you want me to do. Perhaps living with this uncertainty is what you want, just in itself. Help me to know."

Chapter 36

Indicted; Leaving

"Have mercy on me, O Lord,
for I am in distress.
Tears have wasted my eyes,
my throat and my heart.
For my life is spent with sorrow
and my years with sighs.
Affliction has broken down my strength
and my bones waste away.
In the face of all my foes
I am a reproach,
an object of scorn to my neighbors
and of fear to my friends.
Those who see me in the street
run far away from me,
I am like a dead man, forgotten,
like a thing thrown away.
I have heard the slander of the crowd,
fear is all around me . . .
But as for me, I trust in you, Lord . . .
my life is in your hands, deliver me . . . .
Save me in your love."

Psalm 31, Liturgy of the Hours,
Monday Readings

On Tuesday, Dec. 27, I was indicted by the Lorain County Grand Jury late in the afternoon. The newspapers said it would be happening. The grand jury held a secret session. The effect of it being secret was that my attorney was not present to make any statements about the evidence against me. The grand jury only hears the one side in a secret indictment.

For the next days the media, newspapers, radio and TV, carried features about me, with the man who is the other half of the 2 man Elyria police youth bureau saying they had a file four-and-a-half inches thick on me, that his "partner" traveled the state to talk with boys, that this was just "the tip of the iceberg." He said they got one boy to talk and then the others all "came forward."

My picture was shown on TV numerous times, and front page in the two papers in Lorain County and in Cleveland and some other cities; the story was on many radio stations, over and over. Some people in Florida called friends saying they had seen it down there.

It sounded like a classic sex case: plenty of evidence, the investigation continuing, many photos, a sure conviction.

Mary and I were home the night the news broke and could not believe this was happening. What would all our friends say, those we work with? Relatives would have a hard time, people in Cleveland and nearby cities.

An indictment by a grand jury is really a finding of guilt in the eyes of the media and public. It is not meant to be, but it is. When the evening news ended a woman called in a whispering, breathless panic and said she was praying for me. She would not tell her name.

The day after the indictment I went to the court house with my attorney; Mary and I put up our house for bond. Then I drove alone to the local jail, the Correctional Center, to be arrested and booked on charges of 24 misdemeanors of a sexual nature, and one felony, the taking of photos. The misdemeanors were 12 charges of importuning (asking to sexually do something) and then 12 counts of "touching erogenous zones." Thus there were actually two counts for each act, asking and doing.

These were repeated over and over in the newspapers the coming months, often using the words "sexual acts were sought and carried out," implying more than touching.

Implying actual acts of sex, as these words usually mean. Making me look as bad as possible.

The arrest at the jail was done by a deputy I had known since his boyhood, a black man from South Lorain, whom I had helped at times. The booking, taking of information, was done by another deputy whose partner in the room was a former foster parent at Betterway. I saw other deputies I knew and they were friendly.

They took my photo, assigned me a number to hold up, took finger prints, and sent me on my way an hour later. I returned to my Betterway office to begin packing up in boxes I had already gotten ready, anticipating. Later I realized it was the Feast of the Holy Innocents in the liturgy the day I went to jail.

At the jail I had many thoughts. The arresting deputy said he could not believe he was doing what he had to do. He was easy and gentle with me, and I told him to go ahead. I passed the small rooms where I had met with so many people who were incarcerated, some former Betterway kids grown up, others just people who asked me to help them or see them.

Now I was one of them. I had worked in this world so long I was part of it, crossing over the line. I thought of Father Damien, the priest who worked with lepers, one day starting his sermon, "Fellow lepers."

I abandoned myself to God. I had no choice. One priest told me a number of times when I spoke of the media that there was nothing I could do about this, so not to worry about what I could do. That advice came to me many times the next months and helped me to avoid spending the time planning responses or ways I would answer all people. I couldn't do anything about it.

In just a few hours time my pride was gone, I was reduced to a despised person. Until the indictment many people thought there was nothing to the talk, but now, an indictment meant business. Something must be up.

I went to see Bishop Cosgrove to talk. He said my most valuable possession was taken away, my reputation. This is everyone's most valuable possession. My reputation was gone, and I could not do anything about it.

The message to "get out of the way" had come into effect quickly and more painfully than I wanted. But it was effective. I was getting out of the way, literally and figuratively.

I was getting out of my office and had things packed by the end of the week. My last act was to walk through the Beacon Home next to our office to just take a look and say goodbye to anyone who might be there. Two boys and a staff were in and I said goodbye. It turned out that the Welfare Department in Cleveland had sent out a number of workers that afternoon to see if I was really gone. They had been upset by the media coverage and were afraid of what I might do to their youth.

One of these workers saw me around our Beacon group home and reported it to a supervisor and caused a great flurry of concern that I was back. Actually I had not left.

But here I was, the founder of group homes, being hounded out of our very first one. I did leave in haste when I saw the welfare worker and later had to explain why I was still there. Another worker called in a panic, this one from the state, to see if "her boys" were safe at Betterway after what she saw on TV. Her boys had all committed felonies and were bigger than me, but she was in a frenzy for their safety. I had known her for years.

So it went. During all this my face was a permanent red wherever I would go. I was in an embarrassed blush for days.

It was the beginning of the New Years weekend when I left the office with the last load of books and my old Royal typewriter. With the long weekend I didn't have the feeling of really being gone, but the next working day it hit me clearly. For the first time in 23 years I was out of Betterway.

What to do for the coming time, however long it might be?

I cleaned my office at home, going through all the books and organizing them, and picking out some to read again. My office is a converted family room which we also call "the library." There are shelves of books on two walls. The walls are a light paneling, pleasant. I have a long desk along another wall, with shelves facing it with the books I use more often. Two filing cabinets are on either side of the desk.

A picture of our Lady of Guadalupe is to my left, as I sit at the desk. A wooden carved crucifix below it. A woodcut of the

Next to my typewriter area at home. The carved cross from Oberammergau and a partial picture of Our Lady of Guadalupe.

Sacred Heart of Jesus by a German, Walter Mellman, next to that, then the Rouault engraving of the French Worker. On the wall to my right are pictures of Dorothy Day, John Vianney, St. Therese, the head of Christ suffering, and a Mexican peasant woman and child by my friend Jean Charlot from Notre Dame.

Next to that is a large framed batik by a Cleveland artist, a modernistic brown and white cloth called "Ascent." Then a drawing by the artist who does the comic Funky Winkerbean, with a strip done at Betterway. Next a favorite picture given to me by Oberlin College black students who walked and wrote about the trek from down south to up north, and finally, a Japanese print, a small man and a high waterfall.

On the one blank wall behind me, I later put a grouping of Icons.

I got out some books to get started, reading part of Sertillanges' *The Intellectual Life* to refresh ways of organizing my free days to accomplish some things. And I got out the books I thought would help me in this time of crisis.

During all this I was faithful to saying the prayers of the *Liturgy of the Hours* during the day, reciting the rosary, and reading the Bible and biographies or other books.

I had been attending Mass in the morning, often at St. Mary's, sometimes St. Jude's, when I saw the Bishop. Now, with my not working, I asked him if I could attend Mass twice a day, morning and afternoon, and receive Communion both times. He said yes, so I began going to St. Jude's at 8:30 and meeting Mary for Mass at 5:00 at St. Mary's. I would say the Liturgy prayers before and after and this gave a beginning and ending to my day.

Now I had to decide what to do in the middle part.

Prayer

"O Lord, I heard the things they were saying about me and felt crushed. I had no defense. I could not speak. You were helping me get rid of my pride, but it was painful. But better this happen now than enter into the next life with that pride. What a wonderful design of providence in these events."

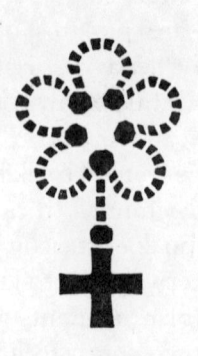

Chapter 37

Writing, Books, Courts, and Funerals

> "God did not make death,
> nor does he rejoice in the destruction of the living . . .
> Though I walk in the valley of darkness, I fear no evil.
> For you are with me Lord."
>
> "Why are you heavy, my heart, why are you so anxious?
> Put your hope in God, for I will praise him still.
> Look on me with love, O Lord, and rescue me."
>
> Liturgy of the Hours,
Office of the Dead,
Daytime Prayers

Filling in the free time.

I scheduled my time for these months that I would be off work, and began some writing. I wrote down everything I could think about in the unfolding of my case, from the details of the first day I knew of the investigation to many other aspects that surfaced later. I wanted to understand what was happening, and why, as best I could. This took 10 days to do, and I had the basic picture, but every once in a while I find out something new.

The next work was really research and writing, on monasteries, and then on genetics, but some other things happened first.

On Jan. 11, I went to court for the first time, to my arraignment. This is a process when a person is read their charges, out loud in front of everyone else being arraigned that day (about 30 people with me) and then the person states a plea (innocent, usually) and a judge is assigned to the case. A person is normally accompanied by an attorney in this.

I arrived in the crowded courtroom and took a seat next to a very nervous young man, about 21, and eventually tried to cheer him up by conversation, though I was nervous too. Twelve men sat chained together in orange jump suits, those who could not afford bond to be out of jail wearing a nice suit like me. The only white man in the chained group trembled so much he could hardly stand up when it was his turn.

People I knew were there, attorneys, photographers, reporters. They took my picture a lot and I tried to look unperturbed. It was over in a half hour and I had my first taste of the coming pretrials and hearings.

That same day I drove over to Lorain with Mary for the Vespers of the Dead for one of my closest friends in my early social work days, Father Leo Rygwalski, who died at age 90. He looked fragile and beautiful in death, in a coffin in the aisle of the church he built for the Polish people of Lorain many years earlier.

The next day I went to his funeral, to the cemetery, and to a Polish lunch in his honor. I was alone, a little embarrassed, saw a lot of priests I knew, heard some talk about me, but enjoyed the meal in Fr. Leo's memory. Over the years we held many dances for street gangs in that same hall. Blacks, Puerto Ricans, Mexicans, Appalachians, none of them Polish. I spent many hours with Father Leo talking over the neighborhood problems.

I felt closer to Father Leo now than ever before.

Books became a very important part of my spiritual formation at this time again. Four were most meaningful: Volume II of the writings of the Spanish Carmelite nun, St. Teresa of Avila, on the inner life. *The Confessions of St. Augustine*, his autobiography. And a book about St. Therese of Lisieux in France. And the poem by Francis Thompson, *The Hound of Heaven*. Other books came later.

Teresa of Avila calls spiritual progress a trip through mansions. She takes a person from basic prayer through detachment from material things, to attachment to God in mystical ways, that is, in ways above our ordinary experiences, feeling a closeness to God even though God is not visible. Like being transported out of this life, sensing a vision, a union. Sometimes we have mystical experiences with a close friend or relative when they have died. We feel their presence, their person.

I was struck by one lesson, where Teresa talked about love of God consisting, not in our happiness, but in our determination to please God in everything we do, to avoid offending him, and to pray for the advancement of his honor and glory on earth.

She said that we must beg God for light to do right, and that he will give us direction and not let us stray. We will eventually attain to the knowledge of the greatness of God, to self-knowledge and humility in realizing how little we are in comparison to God, and we will come to have contempt for earthly things except insofar as they can be used to serve God.

She has many thoughts on the need to become "nothing" in the sight of God and the service of others, so God can work through us. "Get out of the way."

St. Augustine was born in the upper part of Africa in 354 and was an intellectual person. His mother, Monica, prayed that he would be more religious, but he lived the cultivated, fast life of the times, lots of parties, girl friends, drinking. He had a baby by one woman. He was teaching in Milan, after first starting his own school in Rome, when he began to look at Christianity and his life.

He resigned his teaching in the fall of 386 and took time to think. He was baptized the Saturday before Easter in 387, about six months after he quit teaching, at the age of 33. He wrote his most famous book, *The Confessions*, shortly after. Monica died while they were on the way back to Africa.

For the next four years Augustine lived a monastic life and then became a priest, eventually a bishop. *The Confessions* is sometimes wordy and not in the style of today's writing, but it is a classic. In Book 10, chapters 26 and 27 are so beautiful.

"Late have I loved You, O Beauty so ancient and so new, late have I loved You! Behold, You were within and I was without. I was looking for You out there, and I threw myself, deformed as I was, upon those well-formed things which You had made. You were with me, yet I was not with You...You did call and cry out and burst in upon my deafness; You did shine forth and glow and drive away my blindness...You did touch me, and I was inflamed with desire for Your peace." (My own translation).

St. Therese, dead at 23, lived a very different life. At 16 she entered a cloistered Carmelite convent, like the one I used to visit in Columbus, and she stayed hidden till death. I wrote about her earlier in this book. Her spiritual life was strongly alive. She was in love with God and lived this love, hour after hour, in the simplest chores and her relationships with the other sisters, sometimes ornery and funny, like that novitiate year for me. An intense experience in small quarters with a few people.

Her autobiography is simple, a love story, a diary of a soul. She wanted to go out into the world and preach and teach, but she was too sickly, and young, and living in a convent, so she did the next best thing. She asked God to help specific individuals she knew with their problems and missionary work. She took on the sufferings of her world as she learned about them. She told others she would continue to do this after her death.

When she died people by the millions read her life and began to pray to her for help, believing her to be close to God. Prayers would be answered and often a rose, a real rose, would be found by the person who was praying. Hence she is often pictured with roses in her arms. One of her jobs in the convent had been to tend the flowers. She is still called The Little Flower by many. Sister flowers. Sister garden.

The poem, *The Hound of Heaven*, first came into my life as a gift of a little book from my mother in 1950. I was 21: "To Tommy Peters from his darling mother. I think it will mean as much to you as it does to me."

The poem is the story of the hound of heaven, The Lord, pursuing a soul through life, through good and bad, finally clasping the hand of the soul to itself. It is a mystical poem, a love story.

It starts with the soul, a person, speaking:

> *"I fled Him, down the nights and down the days;*
> *I fled Him, down the arches of the years;*
> *I fled Him, down the labyrinthine ways*
> *Of my own mind; and under running laughter.*
> *Up vistaed hopes, I sped;*
> *And shot, precipitated*
> *Adown Titanic glooms of chasmed fears,*
> *From those strong Feet that followed,*
> >   *followed after."*

The Lord keeps up his unrelenting pace for the fleeing soul, finally taking it to Himself near the closing of the poem where the Lord says these words:

> *"How little worthy of any love thou art!*
> *Whom wilt thou find to love ignoble thee,*
> *Save Me, save only Me?*
> *All which I took from thee I did but take,*
> *Not for thy harms,*
> *But just that thou might'st seek it in My arms.*
> *All which thy child's mistake*
> *Fancies as lost, I have stored for thee at home:*
> *Rise, clasp My hand, and come."*

It seemed like the themes of these books were all part of my life at this time: the developments of an inner life according to St. Teresa, the "conversion" of St. Augustine, the simple style of St. Therese, and the pursuit of my soul by the hound of heaven.

Prayer

"You began to lead me along new paths. You began to fill my emptiness with new adventures. O Lord, I was down and you lifted me up. Help me to do that for others who enter my world."

Chapter 38

Oberlin College: Chromosomes and Monasteries.

"Whenever you begin any good work you should first of all make a pressing appeal to our Lord to bring it to perfection . . . for we must always serve him with the good things he has given us . . . There is a good fervor which sets us apart from evil inclinations and leads us toward God and eternal life. Monks should put this fervor into practice with an overflowing love . . . no one should choose what he considers good for himself, but rather what seems good for another."
>Rule of St. Benedict, Liturgy of the Hours,
>Feast of St. Benedict, A Reading.

Oberlin College, part of my growing up, entered my life again. I took out a library card at the Mudd Learning Center, a four story building in the center of the campus, which is also about the center of Oberlin, next to those buildings where my father and I worked. This library quickly became a place to retreat into the world of books, and also a place where I was unknown and enjoyed the excitement of bright, young, students all around.

I had always been curious about the way in which different races and nationalities developed. Why do Scandinavians have blond hair, why can we recognize an Italian, why are Chinese eyes slanted, skin yellowish? Why are blacks black and whites, white. Now I had time to find out.

This led me into the books on genetics, chromosomes, Mendel the monk, and other readings. I went every day until I knew what I wanted, and then wrote some of my Sunday columns on the subject. It was a fascinating crash course. I found out races and looks stem from geography and climate, then genes and chromosomes, interacting over the centuries. Facial and body features and personality traits are then passed from generation to generation to give separate nationality and racial appearances and characteristics. That is the process, but I did not find out why some oriental skin color is yellowish and why their eyes are shaped the way they are.

Next I decided to work on an idea that had been in my mind since that visit to the prison in Lucasville, Ohio, seeing all those Moslem monks at prayer. I would study everything I could on monasteries of all religions. I would write out an idea for a monastic life-style for people other than Moslems, people in prisons or on the outside in halfway houses, nursing homes, shelters. Also for nomadic people living like St. Benedict Joseph Labre, street people.

This took about four weeks of daily work, reading the history and daily schedules of monks in the religions of the world. While I was reading this background I began to write out this idea. I also used my experiences in the novitiate, visits to monasteries, reading the Liturgy of the Hours, and my knowledge of people in prisons and people on the outside. I wanted an idea that would bring the monastic experience into everyday life, like an A.A. meeting brings group dynamics and psychology and religion into everyday life.

The writing went well, the reading was fascinating. I borrowed ideas from my VIA Club book, using a revision of my agenda for those social work gang/club meetings for the new meetings.

The bishop read the parts as I finished them, and then a few other people. I sent some ideas off to my friend, the brother at Gethsemani, the Trappist monastery. Finally I felt it was ready to send off to some chaplains in prisons and I had to settle on a name for my new idea. It ended up being called The Monasteries.

I wrote it up in a lengthy way, with the history of monasteries in all major religions, and the idea for my concept. Then I wrote it up in a popular way and am reproducing that here.

Fr. Raphael, a priest on Rykers Island, New York City's prison, wrote to me after reading it, saying how much prisoners remind him of monks, and monks of prisoners. He had just returned to the prison from a retreat in a Trappist monastery. He invited me to visit him in the prison where he lives.

I hope the idea takes off. Here is a summary of what I wrote in the winter of 1989:

The MONASTERIES
A New Organization, An Old Idea.

Sometimes we hear the phrase, "I'm going to join a monastery."

We think of going off to a mountain place to meditate, pray, and study. To be alone.

The Hindu religion in 1500 B.C. had the first monasteries, and still has them. Men or women live in small groups to think, pray, and study. Buddhism started in 500 B.C. and monasticism is the heart of this religion. Christians started them in the year 280 and they spread rapidly by the year 500, when St. Benedict wrote a famous rule for groups living as monks. In medieval days they were the schools for Europe. People were also sent to them to do penance, and were called penitents.

Why the attraction for monasteries in so many cultures for so many years?

We come into this world alone, and we leave it alone. We all have a need to be alone with our creator, our Lord, at times. The word monk, means alone, separate. To be alone we go on retreats, or take a walk in the woods, by the ocean or a river. Our spirits seem to be free of the pulls of daily problems. We become contemplative. We meditate. We may pray just looking at the beauty around us. We find God. God finds us.

When penitents went to monasteries to atone for sins they too prayed and found God, joining in with the monks schedules and works of charity, caring for the poor.

When the monasteries were too full to take more penitents, governments built penitentiaries, looking and running like monasteries. They had walls, cells, bells, a daily routine, special clothing, simple food, and the key elements of the monastic life: poverty, chastity, and obedience. They had times of silence, daily work, visiting days. Some prisons and monasteries still look alike.

But without the spiritual heart, and study and meditation, penitentiaries lost their sense of peace and reform, and often became very different, with fights, arguments, and even riots. The people became prisoners, not penitents. The clothing a sign of humiliation. The schedule a burden. A place to "do time" and not to do penance.

All people seem to have a need to do penance and to get right with God to be ready for death someday.

Most religions teach that helping others who are needy is the key to salvation. Love of neighbor. This is a getting-ready activity, a type of penance; we will be judged on what we do for others.

Then I wrote about spending a day in a large maximum-security prison and entering a room with 50 men in white robes, praying, Muslims. They were monks, like those I had visited often in the Trappist Monastery at Gethsemani. Monks in prison.

The idea and sight had been in my mind since then, and led to this idea. *The Monasteries.*

This organization or concept will be composed of small groups of people of any age who will meet in chapters like A.A. groups, and who will perform the seven works of mercy: feed the hungry, care for the dying and sick, visit the prisoner, help bury the lonely dead, give drink to the thirsty, clothe the naked, welcome the homeless. They will do this in their spare time or for some, full time. Like monks for thousands of years they will pray seven times a day, from dawn to night, mostly reciting the ancient words of the psalms, just a few minutes each time, trying to follow the schedule of the nearest actual monastery for their prayer life. This can be done privately or as a group, aloud.

In the weekly (or less frequent) meetings they will follow an outline to see how they are doing in their works of mercy and prayer life. Some may choose to live together in a home, maybe taking in the homeless, the hungry, or working in a soup kitchen nearby, or running their own kitchen.

Those who live together will follow some basic rules set down by Benedict and still used in monasteries around the world. I wrote these out in simplified form.

Groups can be formed in penitentiaries and institutions, nursing homes, group homes.

A person can also join *The Monasteries*, who does not attend any meetings, but affiliates with one somewhere in spirit and prayer and work. This could be a homeless person. A nomad. A hermit. One who lives alone without the monastic setting or group or chapter. Such persons have a long history in monasticism in all religions.

There can be special clothing. When doing the works of mercy, or living together, members may wear the garb of the closest prison, or the prison they were in at one time, or may be in now. This is often a "jump suit" of bright color. A sense of shame may be attached to this in prison, but when worn to do acts of mercy the clothing will acquire a sense of dignity, like the white robes of Mother Teresa. An emblem has been designed by Adé Bethune. It has a broken wall and a dove with an olive branch . . . breaking down walls between people, bringing peace.

That's the idea. Small books of psalms are available divided into hours and days of the week. I have the outline for the chapter meetings and a schedule of prayer times in monasteries around the country. A longer paper on this idea is available. The benefits are: 1) restores the monastic penitent spirit to members in prison, 2) enables people outside monasteries to share some of the spirit and life-style of the ancient monastic tradition. 3) It also fosters the works of mercy, and 4) promotes prayer.

Prayer

"O Jesus, learning and expanding the mind is so enjoyable. Thank you for the wonderful library at Oberlin and for helping me bring together so many ideas and experiences in my life to find the Monasteries idea.

"I do not know if any people will like the idea and want to follow it in some form, but as time goes along I will do what I can to promote it. I envision prisons turning again into monasteries, and I see the people in them as capable of becoming monks, alone with you so many times."

Chapter 39

Humiliation and Forgiveness

> "Lord my God, I call for help by day;
> I cry at night before you . . .
> my life is on the brink of the grave.
> I am reckoned as one in the tomb:
> I have reached the end of my strength,
> like one alone among the dead . . .
> You have laid me in the depths of the tomb
> . . . I am drowned beneath your waves.
> You have taken away my friends
> and made me hateful in their sight . . .
> . . . my eyes are sunken with grief.
> . . . to you I stretch out my hands.
> . . . why do you hide your face?
> I have borne your trials; I am numb.
> Friends and neighbor you have taken away;
> my one companion is darkness."
>
> Psalm 88, Liturgy of the Hours,
> Good Friday, Daytime Prayer

As the weeks went on after the indictment my embarrassment and humiliation came and went, depending on what the media and people I met said. Whenever there was a pretrial my case would be covered if the reporters knew about it, and they used sexual references to describe my charges.

Reporters in the courts are in almost daily touch with the police and prosecutors to get "inside" information on cases, so their reporting is often from the prosecutor's viewpoint, rather than the defendant's. No reporter ever talked with me about my feelings or thoughts. During all this I never even met the young reporter who wrote about me in my home town paper, the paper where I had a column for 20 years.

I also never met the detective who worked full time investigating me for months, and did not know what he looked like until he came to a hearing almost a year after he started work on my case. I had never talked to the prosecutor or his assistants either.

At times I had great emotions of embarrassment, anger, frustration, feelings of revenge toward people I had not met, but who were writing and saying all kinds of things about me.

I felt strange to be a focus of people who never sat down face to face to talk, people who lived in my town, just minutes from where I lived, in my boyhood neighborhood.

It is easy to hate such people. I decided that hatred would not be good for me. What to do?

One day I was reciting the Our Father aloud with Bishop Cosgrove at the end of a talk session. We came to the words, "Forgive us our trespasses as we forgive those who trespass against us." It was clear. If I wanted God to forgive me my faults, I had to forgive others. It was suddenly easy and natural, and stayed that way ever since, except for that rare moment when some new development comes along. Even then I get rid of any vengeful feelings in a few moments.

Christ was always forgiving the people who gave him a hard time, right up to death. "Father, forgive them, they don't know what they are doing." He even made excuses for them. He told lots of stories about forgiveness: the prodigal son, the woman caught in adultery, the good thief.

Then there was the embarrassment. It was the season of Lent as I was trying to deal with this in my life. In Lent Catholics and some others try to do extra devotions as a penance to get ready for the joy of Easter. The joy is to be a contrast with the penance and fasting.

I started to "make the stations." This is a devotional experience going back centuries. All Catholic churches have 14 stations, or stopping places, along the inside walls, depicting 14 final events in the life of Christ. Events when he was condemned to death by the local Roman authority, when he carried the wooden piece on which he would be executed, was stripped of his clothes, nailed to his cross, and hoisted up to die and be scorned by the passersby.

In "making the stations," the individual starts by walking to the scene depicting Christ's conviction by the Roman authority, and then walks along all the events to the burial of the dead Christ, meditating and thinking about each of the 14 depicted scenes. The depictions may be paintings, metal or wood sculptures, three dimensional figures, or any other art form.

On his journey of an hour or so Jesus made his way through the narrow streets of Jerusalem, toward a gate leading outside the wall surrounding the city. All condemned criminals who were to be executed walked this way. Crowds gathered for the spectacle just as crowds gather today for any dramatic public event. Crowds made fun of Christ as they did all convicted prisoners. They probably pushed and shoved him. His friends abandoned him and hid out, afraid they too might be tried similarly, or just too embarrassed to be seen as the friend of a convicted criminal. A felon.

When Jesus was going along he is described as falling down under the weight of the wooden bar (probably the crosspiece, say historians, as the up and down part of the cross used in crucifixions was permanently in the ground; condemned prisoners were tied and nailed to the cross bar by the Romans, then hauled up by ropes to die). The soldiers ordered a spectator, a man named Simon, who was a visitor to Jerusalem, to help Jesus carry the wood piece, since he had no friends to help him.

One of the "stations" at the Poor Clare's chapel has a carved depiction of Christ leaning on the arm of Simon, resting his head. I was touched by this image. Christ looks so worn and sad and must lean on this stranger who looked puzzled and sympathetic. His friends were absent.

Another station shows where Christ has his robe taken off in front of the crowd that had gathered to watch the days excitement on the hilltop used for executions. It was a seamless garment, probably made by Mary. The soldiers in authority took it from him and rolled dice for it.

The "stations" at the Franciscan chapel. Jesus leans on Simon who helps him with the wooden beam; Jesus has his clothes torn off before his death. (left to right)

By then a few friends had gathered around, but could only watch as the law took its course. Jesus, naked, or near naked, was fastened to the wooden beam he had carried, with nails and rope, then hauled up by means of another rope with pulleys until he was off the ground and placed in a manner forming a cross, atop the tall beam. In the beginning of my long struggle I often held my carved, wooden crucifix in my hands, thinking how Jesus suffered.

There he hung for the next three hours or so, a spectacle to those who stayed and to strangers passing in and out of Jerusalem on this main highway. And there he died, that most sacred moment in a person's life, death, was public and humiliating to him, and to his loved ones who were watching. His mother was there, John, and a few others.

All of this followed a public scourging, a beating, being mocked as a king, getting spit on, and having a crown of thorny vines pushed into his skin.

Could anyone have it worse? And when we consider the dignity and reality of what we believe about Christ, this is God's son, God the creator of life, the ultimate judge of those soldiers. When we consider this, it is a hundred times more startling. He could have stopped them at any time. He could have gotten even.

But he taught us a lesson. A lesson about what counts. His embarrassment and humiliation and scorn and pain and loneliness and even death were overcome in the glory that was to come in the resurrection. Jesus rose above all this suffering and appeared to his friends a few days later, calling out to the former sinful woman, the first one he wanted to see, "Mary". She understood suffering and joy.

The more I looked at the "stations" and read the gospels on this ordeal, the more I knew my embarrassment was nothing like that. In fact I began to take joy in my suffering, small as it was in comparison. Then there are the words, "Take up your cross, and follow me."

When I made the round of "the stations" in some churches I noticed they were chipped and needed painting or fixing, so I volunteered to do this in a few churches, adding a new skill to my resume: restorer of stations.

Prayer

"O Lord, those seemed like such difficult times. I was staggering with shame. You, my wife, and my family helped me survive. I pray to forgive those who did this. That is the greatest challenge of all, but you have left me an example."

Chapter 40

Icons and Maronites

> "Lord,
> we praise you
> with our lips,
> and our lives and hearts.
> Our very existence is a gift from you;
> to you we offer all that we have and are."
> Liturgy of the Hours, Prayer,
> Saturday Morning

Icons were always a part of my adult devotional life. These are Eastern Rite paintings of God and historic religious events. The faces are bold, direct, often look straight at the viewer and have large eyes.

The features are simple, without the details of a Rembrandt or the blurred color of impressionists. An icon is not like a photograph.

Mary and Jesus are usually done in colors of mostly gold and red with some blue and green. The colors depict royalty. Christ is usually stern, serious, kind, not fooling around. Mary is often pictured with the Christ-child in her arms, the child clinging to the hand and neck of Mary, with the hands unusually small and delicate compared to the head and body.

There is a fragile, mystical, compelling beauty to the icon. They are found in Eastern Rite churches on the walls and in front of the people, sometimes shielding the altar from the public to heighten the sense of a sacred act taking place on the altar. It is too sacred to be seen, like the Holy of Holies. Lots of candles, mostly in red glass, burn around these icons. They are part of the mystique.

In February of 1989 I was reading several books on icons, an easy one by Basil Pennington, a Trappist monk, and a more complex one, The Meaning of Icons, by Leonid Ouspensky and Vladimir Lossky, (published by St. Vladimir's Orthodox Seminary, in Crestwood, New York).

I decided to create my own icon wall at home, in a blank area behind my chair at my desk, to my back as I type. I would put a kneeler here and have a small prayer area, since I could not bring the Eucharist home at that time. I would make a sacred place.

St. Vladimir's Greek Orthodox Seminary sells icons and liturgies on tapes, and books. I ordered icons from them through our Search Shop.

The first to come was a large one, about 17 inches wide and 26 inches high. It represented Christ the teacher, a figure looking straight at me, open book in one hand, and the other raised in the Eastern blessing of a nearly open palm.

I put it on my home office wall, a small table in front of it and then the kneeler, which the pastor at St. Mary's gave me. On the table I placed a large vigil candle in red glass, and hung a small candle with a brass chain next to the icon. When I can, I read the Liturgy of the Hours here, kneeling. Christ seems present.

Next eight smaller icons came in the mail, about 12 inches by 16 inches high. They went along the same wall in groupings: one depicting the Last Supper, another the transfiguration of Christ, when he shone in glory in front of his friends. One was of the resurrection, the coming of the Holy Spirit on the early church, the "falling asleep" or dormition of Mary, a gaunt John the Baptist, a larger icon of the crucifixion, and one I could not figure out, but I ordered it because I liked the scene of people walking in procession.

I added a blue glass-enclosed candle to the table and two five inch icons of Mary and Jesus, and waited for a large one of

The icon wall in my library-office at home, with the kneeler from St. Mary's.

Mary I had ordered. When it came, the wall was filled and is a joy to me every day. I light the candles on special feasts and at prayer.

It took a phone call to the seminary to find out the meaning of the icon with all the people surrounding a wall. It celebrated the saving of Constantinople from the Persians in 626, part of the Akathistos Hymn lore. That made it perfect for me, a nice surprise.

Later when we turned some of the Betterway homes into places for adults, I painted one wall red in the living rooms of some and hung copies of the two large icons of Jesus and Mary on these walls, with candles nearby. These have become important in the homes, a place for refuge, a prayer wall. The same seminary was the source of tapes of Byzantine and Orthodox music and I play it in the car and at home. One tape from a Japanese Byzantine liturgy is especially haunting.

There is one more story in the Eastern end of spirituality in my life. One day when I was on leave from Betterway I went into the market area of Cleveland and then to a place to buy Lebanese bread, The Middle East Bakery. Next door is a church with a sign, Maronite Catholic Church. I had seen the building hundreds of times, but knew it only as a nicely shaped brick church and a hall for bingo next door.

When I arrived at the bakery a big black hearse and a line of big black cars pulled up before the church, heading a very long funeral procession. People stepped out from the big cars and the smaller cars, dressed in oldworld style black clothes; all were somber faced. It reminded me of a scene from "The Godfather." I was free to do what I wanted that day so I decided to go to the funeral.

I like funerals in the Catholic tradition and knew this would be interesting, since the people looked somewhat foreign, Middle Eastern. It was a wonderful funeral and a wonderful liturgy. There were a number of priests in gold robes, plus incense bearers, and when I walked inside, a full church. The building had a gold and green interior, regal looking. It had a vaulted, domed ceiling, like a mosque.

A woman cantor, sometimes two, were wailing in loud and sad voices, weeping as described in the gospels when Lazarus was dead, or the important official's daughter, wailing and weeping and gnashing of teeth.

The music was oriental, making me think of belly dancing sounds, with drums and high pitched noises. The funeral was long, with many words of praise for the matriarch who had died, the mother of some families in the front rows, a pillar in her Lebanese community and church. I received communion by tincture, where the bread is dipped into the wine and then placed on the tongue. The chanting and prayers were in English at times, other times in Arabic and a few times Aramaic, the language Jesus spoke.

I had never heard Aramaic before and was thrilled to hear how it sounded. I decided to study about the Maronites and return to the church some Sundays.

Back home I read about this religion found mostly among the Lebanese, scattered in a few areas of the world, and in Lebanon. Many of the parishioners were business people in

Cleveland, like the owners of the bakery next door. Some looked a little like they were out of the movies, dark skin, curly or straight jet black hair, exotic looking women. They smiled and knew one another and were a close-knit, happy group, even at a funeral.

I read up on the religion and the liturgy; one part of the Mass that is in Aramaic is the offertory procession, which is very dramatic. It proceeds around the inside of the church for all to see, with the solemn beat of drums and organ and Aramaic singing. Aramaic is used again after the consecration of the bread and wine. The other parts of the Mass are English, or Arabic, the language of the Lebanese.

Mary and I returned a few weeks later on a Sunday. The music was even better and we found out some instruments are not used in funerals, when the music is not as exuberant as on Sundays.

We went there several times and plan to continue to go. I feel great excitement to hear the Aramaic language Christ spoke, and to hear the music. Music Jesus knew to sing psalms, to pray to his father, to dance at weddings, like Cana, to lament at funerals, to sing childhood songs. The music in Israel had to sound much like this ancient Maronite Rite.

I saw the whole thing as a gift from the Lord and as a way of drawing me closer to Jesus. When I read the gospels or the Old Testament and find references to the music of those times I think of St. Maron's Church.

This experience at this time in my life was a great comfort.

Prayer

"Lord, I begin to see the value in all this. The beauty of icons grows in my spiritual life, the beauty of the Maronite rite and hearing your own music and language is so wonderful. Perhaps these things would not have entered my life if it had not been for the troubles of these days. I should be thanking those who were part of this all."

Chapter 41

More Books: *The Last Things*; The *Song of Songs*

> "I called to the Lord in my distress
> he answered and freed me.
> The Lord is at my side; I do not fear.
> What can man do against me?
> The Lord is at my side as my helper . . .
> I was hard pressed and was falling
> but the Lord came to help me.
> The Lord is my strength and my song;
> he is my savior."
>
> Psalm 118, Liturgy of the Hours,
> Sunday Morning Prayer

Two more books came into my life's spiritual journey in 1989.

About this time, in Lent, I found a book on my shelves called *The Last Things*, by a writer popular in my seminary days, Romano Guardini, an Italian priest.

It was on death, purification after death, resurrection, judgment, and eternity, all in 118 pages.

Death and the afterlife have been of interest to me since I was 19 and had that experience of nearly dying in the cemetery in Dayton. I had weeks in that oxygen tent in the hospital to wonder where I would be if I had died. In the schooling that followed, I read Garrigou-Lagrange and Scheeben on the subject, and later Kubler-Ross and all her books on death and dying, although hers are on the process of death, rather than the theology of the next life. I taught college courses on the act of dying, using Kubler-Ross's books.

Along with this has been my longtime fascination with cemeteries, walking through them and realizing that all these stones mark the burial places of people who were alive like I am now. And that someday I will be gone from this earth, like them.

Thoughts come to me on death when I am at "big crowd" events like at a stadium, with thousands of people, and I think how all of them will be dead in less than a hundred years, many less than 50 years. When I see long lines of people waiting to get in some place, like a model home or a movie, I think of how they will be lined up to pass into heaven or hell at judgment (even though I know there is no line).

When I see crowds rushing to and from work in a big city I think of how all these people will soon be gone, soon, in the light of the quickly passing centuries of time.

When my mother went to a nursing home for awhile I saw people just barely alive, fastened to machines, unable to talk or move, skin and bones. Yet they were alive, on the verge of going away into death. When we visit Florida we are in death's waiting room for many people. Like a giant doctor's office.

At a busy airport I see the elderly, gray haired people rushing and rushing, and then I imagine them in nursing homes, the same people, so still and tired, then in their coffins. No more rushing to catch or meet a plane.

When I go to a wake and look at a deceased person I wonder where they are, what they are doing and thinking. I talk with them in my mind.

This little book by Guardini, *The Last Things*, is one I go to regularly. It helps me understand that death is a result of sin, it is our last venture on earth, our last act.

I got these further ideas: if we are not wanting to meet God, our creator, our Lord, it will be because we are too attached to some things in life yet: our possessions, a person, pride and self importance, a bad habit. While living we can weed these things out, but after death we leave the time to do that behind us. There is no more time to do good and avoid evil. All of our inner thoughts will be exposed, our deepest secrets, smallest lies.

If we are not ready to meet God, these things will be burned out of us through suffering, the same kind of suffering we sometimes experience on earth: loneliness, a feeling of loss, separation, and pain of some kind, to free us of attachments to this world. When we suffer great pain, we do not desire anything like a new car, or "getting even," or good looks. The pain cleans us out, purifies us, purges us. Theology calls pain in the next life, purgatory, purging. People in nursing homes know.

In the resurrection of the body, our body and soul will be joined again to make us our real self to live in everlasting life. As I wrote earlier, I am not fully "me" unless I have my body, and it will be a body showing all the stages of my life, babyhood, teen years, adulthood, old age. People die at all those various ages, even babies in the womb, but in the resurrection they will somehow be whole, full, entire, all their ages.

Judgment: presented simply in the gospel, it is based on how we treat our neighbor. "I was sick and you visited me." "Come, blessed, into my kingdom." I was hungry, a stranger, naked, in prison, and you came to me. There is nothing high and mighty about judgment. It is what we did for others in our lifetime. Not the endless prayers we said, not our wisdom, our power, our wealth. Simply what we did for others, or did not do.

Then there is eternity. When life ends, history for each has come to its conclusion. The creature is united in communion with the Creator, with God. It is a shocking idea, never ending, eternal. If one is too attached to sin, to self-indulgence, to selfishness, and never did give to the hungry and all, then one is stuck in eternal damnation, eternal despair, eternally missing the chance to love God, to love friends, to love.

One can only hate. Hate oneself for ending up this way, and hate everyone else for not preventing it. We have all experienced this self hatred when we have done something wrong.

But then we pick ourselves up and make it right and go on, unless we give up on ourselves and God. That is hell: agonizing despair and hate.

There was a powerful ending to this small book by Guardini: God the Father's relationship to the Son, through the Holy Spirit, is the essence of God. God is relating. God is love, loving someone else. When we enter eternity, we enter this loving relationship between the Father, Son, and the bond, the Spirit. All are persons. This is why we are judged by how we loved persons on this earth. If we loved persons (feed the hungry, etc.) we will be ready to enter the loving Trinity of Father, Son, Spirit.

If we do not know how to love, we will be alone. And being alone is hell too.

I think God left me isolated to some degree to empty me of self love to make room for others, for Himself.

The second book in my life in Lent was really two, The *Song of Songs* from the Old Testament, and a book about the *Song of Songs* called *The Cantata of Love*, a verse by verse commentary, gathered from many authors, by Blaise Arminjon, a Jesuit.

Somewhere during Lent I read some thoughts on the *Song of Songs* and decided to read this poem on some special occasion. One Thursday I took the Bible with me to pray at Lorain's Sacred Heart and spent the hour reading the *Song* slowly, some parts over and over.

It is not really a song between two human lovers, as it seems at first, but between a person, the bride, us, and the Lord, the groom. It is another way of saying what *The Hound of Heaven* says, and St. Augustine's "Too late have I loved You." I do not think I ever read the *Song of Songs* this way before, and it seemed so beautiful that day that I wanted to learn more of its meaning. I had just read a review of a new book out from Ignatius Press and started to read it as soon as it came in at our store. It was, *The Cantata of Love*.

The commentaries, verse by verse, are by many spiritual writers, including Augustine, St. Therese, John of the Cross, St. Bernard, Chouraqui, St. Francis de Sales, others.

In the *Song of Songs* the bride sings, "I hear my Beloved, see how he comes, leaping on the mountains, bounding over the hills."

"Come then, my love, my lovely one, come, for see, winter is past, the rains are over and gone, the flowers appear on the earth, the season of glad songs has come . . . come then my love, my lovely one, come."

The bridegroom speaks: "Come from Lebanon, my promised bride, come from Lebanon, come on your way . . . you ravish my heart, my promised bride."

The bride and the groom pursue one another all through the poem, never catching up. There was a great lesson in this for me, one I had not grasped yet in life.

We are always pursuing our lover, the Lord, and we never catch up to him in this life. He is always around the corner, in the mist, across the mountain. We will never rest in this pursuit in this life.

Previously I thought someday I would obtain peace here, everything would be all right, in place, orderly, done, no more struggle, no more pursuit.

But this is not the way it is. We must get up each day and continue the chase. The Beloved is just ahead. There is no time to rest.

"See where he stands, behind our wall, he looks in at the window . . . my dove, hiding in the clefts of the rock, in the coverts of the cliff, show me your face.

"On my bed at night I sought him, whom my heart loves. I sought him but did not find him. So I will rise and go through the city; in the streets and the squares I will seek him whom my heart loves, . . . I sought but did not find him."

Life is a continual seeking. There is no retirement in this pursuit, no day to sit back, no stopping love.

Prayer

"Lord, you continued to enrich my mind with thoughts about this life and the next. I love to think about eternity and death. I love to pray the Song of Songs. I could say the words over and over and never tire of them.

"Thank you for all of this."

Chapter 42

Return to Betterway

"I love the Lord for he has heard
the cry of my appeal;
for he turned his ear to me
in the day when I called him.
. . . I was helpless so he saved me
. . . I will walk in the presence of the Lord
in the land of the living."

> Liturgy of the Hours,
> Friday evening Prayer

When the police investigation started, the Betterway board hired an attorney to advise them and he hired a private investigating firm to interview all the people the detective was seeing, plus more, to find out if there were grounds for charges against me.

Two former Cleveland policemen were assigned to the job in the Fall of 1988. By the spring of 1989 they talked to the board's attorney and the attorney told our board there was no reason that I could not return to Betterway. To avoid upsetting the agencies placing youth at Betterway, our board decided to have me return as director of adult programs. I was to fill the three empty group homes. They were empty because the agencies usually placing boys and girls at Betterway had mostly stopped doing so, although they did leave their kids there who were already in placement. The natural departure of youth that we always experienced at Betterway resulted in the empty homes, since no new ones came.

On April 20, I returned, the feast of Passover. I did a column in the local paper on having "passed over" the most difficult time in my life, and compared it to the Passover of the Jewish people from Egypt to the promised land. My four months away were over.

I had already been developing some ideas for the use of these empty homes, namely as places for people without homes, the homeless. One home for women, one for men, and one for small families or women with babies and children. These would be homes, not shelters, where a person could stay as long as necessary. There would be no staff and they would be self-governing, with help from Betterway. Bills like utilities, house payments, insurance, would be paid by the people living there, from jobs, welfare, social security.

In reality we would be providing a physical, furnished place to live, and the people living there would provide the everyday expenses and what might be called the program, or way of living.

Another social agency already had funds to provide a "shelter" in the community, with staff, a limited 30 day stay, and rules of living: door locked at certain times, etc. I did not want to have that type setup. I do not see it as a solution to the homeless problem. I met some men who went from shelter to shelter across the country, staying the time limit, usually 30 days in each. They were nomadic vagabonds, generating tons of paperwork in local hospitals and welfare departments and social agencies. Then moving on to the next closest city, never attaining roots or stability.

I felt people needed a sense of community among themselves and then in the town. I visited programs in Cleveland and had seen similar places over the years. The ones I liked the most were the Catholic Worker houses, which are more permanent, like I envisioned, but do have volunteers who are like staff. In my visiting I found all kinds of shelters and living places, including those with the name "transitional," which generally means a year or so, but not permanent.

The "not permanent" idea is big in the shelter world, and in some places the first thing the person is told is that they can only stay 30 days. They must go out job hunting between one and four in the afternoon when the doors are locked and all must go, children too. What a strange way to welcome someone, telling them how long they can stay, when they must go. We would never welcome people in our own house this way, and if we did, and they had any sense of dignity, they would leave. The fact that people do not leave such programs means they have no dignity or must swallow their pride out of need, which makes them all the more beat-down and unable to function. No wonder so many never get on their feet.

When I came back to work at Betterway the media picked up on it and wrote about my charges, the indictment, repeating the sexual wordings of the charges. One newspaper published a long editorial critical of our board for bringing me back and sympathetic to all the boys who had the courage to come forward and tell what I had done. Our board had simply said they were bringing me back to work with adults and that I was good at creating new programs.

When I wrote about the idea for the new programs in my Sunday column to get donations of furniture and food, some city officials and councilmen reacted hastily, saying Elyria did not need homes for homeless, they would be flophouses, and they would be investigated and stopped if possible.

Sensing the possibility of legal action to stop our opening, I moved rapidly and on May 5, 1989, opened the Beacon Home, our original one, for men. I mentioned it in my column as being ready and spread the word around town. Five men came in a week, one having heard about it from his "shelter" under a much used bridge over the Black River.

The former Ark Home opened a week later for families and women with babies, and about four weeks later the Search Home opened for women. We kept the names we had been using for years for each home. City officials called me in for an unfriendly meeting on what we were doing, but we continued.

As with any new idea there were rough spots, but everyone is forever learning how to deal with them. The men's home was almost always full after we opened, the family home could have been filled three times over. The women's was not filled at first, but as the word got around that we took pregnant single women, this changed.

Being in a new kind of "program" and returning to work at Betterway brought new challenges into my life. I no longer had the free time to pray as much whenever I wanted. I developed a new schedule to continue those things since they had become an essential part of my life. This included the reading, and some time set aside in the morning for writing.

It also meant spending time in the early evening in one of the new homes, because people were working or busy during the day and could not meet as a whole group. I felt this was necessary to get a sense of community and of caring for the house and for one another. I knew that people living on the streets, in cars, under bridges do, in fact, care for one another, but in a basic kind of way. Coming to rescue one another in times of trouble with the police, or when one person is sick and needs emergency care, or is too drunk and needs to sleep it off in a hidden place, or needs belongings packed up in an abandoned house when they are arrested and taken to jail or a ride to the free meal that night, or the food distribution center. It takes a lot of caring and planning to get through each day when one does not have a home. It is something most people could not do if told to try it for a week.

It is pure myth that a street-living person is all lazy or drunk all the time or filthy. In my view, it takes more skill to survive that way, a day-by-day struggle, than it does the way most of us go through life, returning to our safe house, our own restroom, a refrigerator, our shower, our bed, plus a phone, electricity, heat, water, and a mail box to get letters. I sometimes sit and think about living without those things. No wonder some people do petty crimes to land in jail for awhile.

While all this was happening with the adult homes, my case had its pretrials, its publicity, but Mary and I went away for an interesting weekend to find dead relatives.

Prayer

"I returned to Betterway and to the tasks ahead. I was mostly emptied of my old self. I scarcely knew what to do. I just started out with what I had . . . empty homes and people in need. You seemed to be leading me, Lord."

Chapter 43

Visiting the Dead and the Not so Dead

"Calling the saints to mind arouses in us a longing to enjoy their company, so desirable in itself. We long to share in the citizenship of heaven, to dwell with the spirits of the blessed. When I think of them, I feel myself inflamed by a tremendous yearning."

From a Sermon of St. Bernard, Abbot
Liturgy of the Hours,
Feast of All Saints, Reading

On the weekend of June 24-25, 1989, Mary and I went to southwestern Ohio, by the Indiana border, around Lake St. Mary's, a mostly German farming area. A few months earlier we had a short visit and a first time sampling of this part of Ohio, and then learned that some of my father's and mother's relatives were from there. The relatives did not know one another back then.

I wrote about some of these connections earlier in this book. During that first visit, when Mary went to see a fabric factory, we were visiting the Maria Stein shrine near Lake St. Mary's and met a woman who was visiting her sister, a nun. She was stationed in this Swiss-German convent, founded to work with the new German immigrants settling in the area around Minster, Ohio. She told us to come back for the local festival in June and stay at her bed-and-breakfast place in Celina, nearby.

Talking with her, we found her brother had married the daughter of Ben Wimmers, brother of my grandfather Hubert, both now dead. We were amazed to find any living relatives in this area. I had read in my family history that they settled there when coming from Germany. We ate in a Minster restaurant and heard some locals talking and asked them about the Wimmers name and they knew a Wimmers in town. We decided to return someday and go relative hunting.

Meanwhile I found out my father's side was also from the area, Lightsville, about 20 miles away. They were English, not part of the German farming immigrants.

Germans came to the area because they arrived in Cincinnati, from Germany, wanted to farm, and took the Toledo canal boat north, getting off in flat farmland, and giving the landing spot the name Minster, really Munster, a German city.

They settled on roads west of Minster, building up beautiful farms, still going today, and big brick churches, German-American Gothic in design, every mile or so at every crossroad. Priests came from a nearby German seminary to serve them, so there were plenty for each parish.

Ever since our first trip I had been thinking about returning. It was almost a calling.

By now I was feeling fairly isolated and separated from the people with whom I normally worked and saw around town. A lot of people in the community did not know what to say when they saw me, so it was easier for me not to be out and about. It had been almost a year since I was under investigation, almost eight months of regular media exposure. When people did talk with me, it was about concerns of their own or the weather or some small problem. I probably seemed disinterested.

My family was one of my main supports and even there I was not as free, as joking, as eager to know what they were doing. An indictment and preparation for a trial casts a pall, a cloud, over life. On the other hand, I seemed to be driven more and more deeply into a spiritual world. It seemed like the saints I admired and read about were closer to me. I relied almost completely on our Lord for strength and ideas in going through the days of sitting in the courthouse, of people speaking to me, people not speaking. We left all this on a weekend away.

We stayed at that bed-and-breakfast place, Das Winklejohn Haus, and got to know the two sisters of the nun at Maria Stein. One was a genealogy fan and had the Mormon family history book almost filled out on the Wincklejohns and their kin. They knew a lot about the Wimmers clan, and had visited Wimmers people in the original log cabin built by my great, great, grandparents Godfred and Eva, when they came from Germany. We had never known the name of Godfred's wife, and here were people who had visited in their log cabin.

We got copies of maps from the land journals at city hall and found entries of the original Wimmers properties, then how they had been sold, and where the one Wimmers farm still was. All lived in the town of St. Henry, a mile from one of those great brick churches, and are buried in the cemetery back of the church.

We drove to the farm properties and took pictures and will visit all the Wimmers clan sometime. We also learned the Wimmers clan and Tobe clan intermarried, and Mary's family name is spelled Tobey and Toby and probably Tobe, from Indiana. We found a lot of Tobe markers in the cemetery, near Wimmers. It seemed like a small world.

Then we headed south to the Lightsville area for my father's family. The German farms changed to regular Ohio farms, without the distinctive brick houses modeled on the Maria Stein convent house, nor the scrupulously neat yards and barns of the Germans.

Along Highway 49 I saw a sign, Peters Road, and in just a little more, Light Road. My great grandfather Myron Peters had married Caroline Elizabeth Light and they must have lived near here. We drove for a few miles down the country gravel roads but found no signs with these names, and were in Indiana when we turned around and went back to the main highway.

Continuing on towards Lightsville, we passed an unnamed cemetery, tombstones on both sides of the road. We turned and drove back to this cemetery and started walking around. I

My great-great grandparents, Myron Harrison Peters and his wife, Caroline Light Peters. Photo taken Feb. 22, 1931 on their 65th anniversary. In 1862, at age 17, Myron joined the Union Army and fought in the Civil War. He was living in Lightsville, Darke County, Ohio. He guarded the casket of Lincoln when it passed through Ohio April 29, 1865. He was the father of Clyde, the father of my father.

found nothing on my side of the road. Mary called out to me to come to the back of the cemetery on her side. There were old markers with the names of Elder Mahlon Peters, the father of Myron who was the father of Clyde, the father of my father. We found Absolom Peters, and others, all relatives. We took pictures and wrote down dates, Elder Mahlon Peters, born in 1791, dying in 1868.

Here we were in the homeland of some of my people. I can't describe the joy and kinship I felt. I could have stayed for hours to savor the experience and I still like to think of it.

Later Bishop Cosgrove commented that they were waiting for me.

Myron and Caroline Peters, and Absolom, and others, in the cemetery outside Lightsville in Darke County, Ohio.

I needed them at this time in my life. That is the communion of saints between the living and the dead. I think we all experience this at times.

We drove into Lightsville, just a few houses and a sign, then down a side road and another cemetery, with a section of Light tombstones, but none I knew, no Great-Grandmother Caroline. This was the burial ground of my great-grandmother's people. She had to have come here for many a funeral, standing on this grass. She is probably buried near her husband, Myron Peters, but we could not find her stone at that first cemetery.

We drove into Greenville, the Darke county seat, and got into their journals and found land markings for numerous Peters and Light people, including those on the Light and

Peters roads and some in Lightsville. Maps from 1857, 1875, and 1910, all with Peters properties, but changing locations and first names over the years.

We made copies of the maps and bought a new county map. We found some history on Greenville and learned that a major Indian treaty had been signed there.

It was wonderful to get away, to meet new living and dead people, and to come home refreshed. Even in death my relatives were helping out, taking care of a family member. And Mary's too, for an additional joy. The Tobes.

I think it was providential that we learned about this settlement of relatives on both sides of my family in just the past year and were led to visit their worlds, their stamping grounds, their churches, their friends.

That evening we sat in our room at Das Winklejohn Haus and I read aloud from Psalm 23. We had just returned from a long walk around the still, quiet waters of Grand Lake St. Marys at dusk.

> The Lord is my shepherd;
> there is nothing I shall want.
> Fresh and green are the pastures
> where he gives me repose.
> Near restful waters he leads me,
> to revive my drooping spirit.
> He guides me along the right path;
> he is true to his name.
> If I should walk in the valley of darkness
> no evil would I fear.
> You are there with your crook and your staff;
> with these you give me comfort.
> You have prepared a banquet for me
> in the sight of my foes.
> My head you have anointed with oil;
> my cup is overflowing.
> Surely goodness and kindness shall follow me
> all the days of my life.
> In the Lord's own house shall I dwell
> for ever and ever.

Prayer

"O Lord, I was so happy to find the burial places of my relatives. They came into my life when I needed them. I have always enjoyed hearing about them, but now they were so much more real. I pray to them to watch over the members of their family who remain on this earth until we join them in heaven. Thank you for bringing us together in those little cemeteries in the countryside of Ohio."

Chapter 44

The Wheels of Justice

"Lord Jesus, love and truth of the Father, you came to earth to relieve the pain of our exile; you took our weakness as your own. Uphold us when our hearts grow faint, until we stand with you before God and praise your name."

Psalm prayer, Liturgy of the Hours,
Saturday Daytime Prayer

My legal case was moving along slowly and we had a hearing when the judge and prosecutor and my attorney came to an agreement to offer me a plea bargain. This is when the defendant (me) admits to being guilty of something, and has a good idea of the penalty to be imposed, (but no written agreement).

I entered a plea of guilty to the photo felony, to end the trial process, in exchange for dropping the 24 misdemeanors and receiving a suspended sentence. The media played this up, emphasizing that I was guilty, downplaying the dropped charges.

This made me feel even worse in the community. People who might have doubted my guilt now said I must be guilty, not understanding the plea bargain process. I explained to some, but to little avail. I now felt even more cut off from people, and I was not sure I should have entered the plea. Further, it was done on July 3, the feast of St. Thomas the

Apostle, my namesake; he is known as the doubting Thomas because he did not believe a risen Jesus had been seen by the other apostles. I was a doubting Thomas now.

On Friday, July 28 I was to be sentenced. The area media and TV were there before 8 in the morning. The day before this we heard that some people might be there to publicly pressure the judge into sentencing me to prison. With legal advice, I decided to withdraw the plea and go to trial. Sure enough, the detective showed up with a boy named in the indictment who had just gotten out of jail.

On Wednesday July 5, the person I gave my Sunday column to at the local newspaper called and said they did not want them anymore, after 20 years of publishing a well-read weekly column. No explanation was ever given in the paper and some people wondered why I had stopped writing. I missed that communication with people very much and later took out paid advertising space for a shorter column on Betterway happenings.

Another "small world" incident: in my new "free time" I became a volunteer at the 300 bed Elyria Methodist Home, just a block from our Betterway office. I had my first day, being introduced around by another volunteer. I asked for the floor of the sickest people since I was told most volunteers did not like this area. The people rarely talked and seemed so hopeless.

The third patient he took me to see was a black man who had suffered a heart attack and lay in bed, mouth open, moaning, no recognition of anyone. He was from our area, Lorain, whereas many patients in this facility were from other parts of Ohio. His name was the same last name as the detective who had done all the investigating on me. Could this be his father? A relative?

I was startled to see this patient because he seemed so "out of it" but more startled to hear his name. I decided he was there for me to find out if I had really set my anger aside. He could be the detective's father. Over the coming weeks I stroked his head and hand, talked with him, and told stories about the good fishing places in Lorain along Lake Erie. He would stop his moaning when I would talk about fishing and rub his head, and once he smiled over the name of "Hot Waters" a good fishing place known to many people. The man died during my trial year and his obituary did not list any relatives I recognized. He was not the detective's father.

Another of the unusual twists about my case was that the detective was black. This bothered me at first, because I had spent years trying to hire blacks, to help in this cause, and my wedding had all black VIA Club boys as ushers. At times I have felt more black than white, and white people would taunt me as a "nigger lover." I have had people in audiences yell at me when I gave speeches on racism.

Besides being black, the detective was a policeman, and I have always enjoyed my dealings with police. I knew a number of them well in Elyria, several became policemen because of my help somewhere along the line, and I taught in police science in two colleges. A number of times the police and I had wild episodes with drunk, angry kids; other times I helped the police solve crimes.

The prosecutor on my case was Jewish. I had to get over any feelings about him as a Jew, because Jews and Judaism are important in my life, related spiritually through my religion, and physically through Eva Wimmers, that French foundling who came to Minster, Ohio.

It is easy to lump people into "like and dislike groups."

On August 2, 1989, the Betterway Board met and after much discussion the majority voted to return me as director. Then the board decided to allow the assistant director of Betterway to try to form a separate corporation with a separate board, a whole new agency, to take over the group homes for youth and the foster homes. Betterway, with me as director, would be out of the youth-serving business. I might develop new programs for adults, in the areas of the homeless, perhaps a maternity home, and a program for dying people.

Ordinarily it might have made me feel excited to be coming back as director, but I was too emptied out to feel much of anything. Besides I had a trial coming up.

The Lord said he came to wash the feet of others, to serve, not to be someone important with a big title and big feeling.

Emily Dickinson said in one of my favorite poems:

> I'm nobody! Who are you?
> Are you nobody, too?
> Then there's a pair of us...don't tell!
> They'd banish us, you know.
>
> How dreary to be somebody!
> How public, like a frog
> To tell your name the livelong day
> To an admiring bog!

Prayer

"This part of my life began to draw to one of its endings, although in some ways there was to be more of the same as another part began. Now I felt I was just swept along by the events that happened. Nothing much was in my control. I was getting out of the way, whether I wanted to or not. Thank you Lord for letting this happen."

Chapter 45

Endings and Beginnings

"There is cause for rejoicing here. You may for a time have to suffer the distress of many trials; but this is so that your faith, which is more precious than the passing splendor of fire-tried gold, may by its genuineness lead to praise, glory, and honor when Jesus Christ appears. Although you have never seen him, you love him, and without seing you now believe in him, and rejoice with inexpressible joy touched with glory because you are achieving faith's goal, your salvation."

1st Letter of St. Peter,
Liturgy of the Hours,
Monday of Easter Week, First Reading

The investigation of me began on August 8, 1988. It is August 4, 1989, as I type this chapter.

Today is the feast of St. John Vianney, the French priest, the Cure d'Ars, born in 1786, died in 1859. He was a parish priest, had bad grades in school, did poorly in Latin (all classes in the seminary were in Latin), but he was finally ordained a priest and became very popular in his little parish church in the country. He had to stay in the confessional half the day to see all the people who wanted to talk with him.

He was a humble, quiet, "nobody" kind of person. Insignificant.

He has been dead 130 years now, not long in the whole span of time. He lived 73 years. Not long either. Forty-one years ago

I read the story of his life and wanted to become a priest too. John Vianney inspired me. I too went off to study like he did. I did not have a hard time with grades or with Latin, and I learned a lot about the same things he did, theology, philosophy, counseling, listening, pastoring, being a shepherd to people.

But I did not get ordained. I did not become a parish priest. I do not spend hours in a confessional, but I do hear "confessions." Lots of them. I spend a lot of time listening to the problems of people.

Sometimes I look at everyday people and wish I could be like them: going fishing, playing golf, a member of some clubs, Rotary, Kiwanis, Knights of Columbus.

But that's not me. I am happiest in the world of the underdogs, the have-nots, the nobodies, those with problems, those suffering.

I have lived 60 years. They went so fast. I do not know if I will live to the 73 of the Cure d' Ars or perhaps longer. But I do

Another wall in my office at home: St. John Vianney, the Cure of Ars on the left, Dorothy Day below, St. Therese (the Little Flower) on the right, and a favorite picture of Christ.

know it will end for me and for everyone around in such a short time. Then we will enter that world where many I have written about in this book have gone. Eternity: mysterious and unsure for now, but soon to become reality. I do not know how my remaining years on this earth will be lived.

I do not know how the wonder of the events I am in will go. They seem so overwhelming at times.

When I appeared in court for that first sentencing, the one that did not happen, I was with my wife and attorney, and saw people I knew, reporters, photographers, citizens. One reporter said hello, and the boy who had been brought in by the detective to speak against me said hello. Everyone else looked at me or looked away, but said nothing. A year ago most of these same people would have been friendly, greeting me.

Now I was a media event, like the person to be hung in the town square in earlier days. Someone who makes the day a little more exciting. Sometimes there is a perverse satisfaction in seeing a person in misery, like watching a fire, an accident.

But I did not get sentenced. Everyone seemed disappointed. They would not hear the words, see my look. They did not know I was looking at them too, with just as much interest.

A poem by Emily Dickinson expresses my feelings:

> The show is not the show,
> But they that go,
> Menagerie to me
> My neighbor be,
> Fair play . . . Both went to see.

I will end this part of the story of my soul with a few selections from *The Liturgy of the Hours* the past days.

The day that the Betterway Board met to consider reinstating me and to decide on the future of Betterway and the staff, I was wondering what I would say, how I would act. That morning I came on this reading in the liturgy: "Do to no one what you yourself dislike. Give to the hungry some of your bread, and to the naked some of your clothing. Seek counsel from every wise person. At all times bless the Lord God, and ask him to make all your paths straight and to grant success to all your endeavors and plans."

That night our Board approved another agency to carry on the youth work started at Betterway, and restored me to my job as director. Everyone was happy with this act of Solomon, seemingly splitting the baby without hurting it.

I was relieved to see an end to my part in the group home world. We were the first anywhere to have such homes, these alternatives to sending boys and girls off to big institutions. Many other cities and states and countries have started group homes in communities, and the institutions have been reformed to become more humane so the whole youth serving world is different. Still it is good that the work we did start may continue and the kids at Betterway will continue to have places to stay, to live, to finish growing up, to love and to be loved.

****

My thoughts at this time leading into the trial were expressed in selections from Psalm 35, used in the *Liturgy of the Hours* for morning on the feast of St. John Vianney:

> O Lord, plead my cause against my foes;
> fight those who fight me.
> Take up your buckler and shield;
> arise to help me.
>
> O Lord, say to my soul:
> "I am your salvation."
>
> But my soul shall be joyful in the Lord
> and rejoice in his salvation.
> My whole being will say:
> "Lord, who is like you
> who rescue the weak from the strong
> and the poor from the oppressor?"

Lying witnesses arise
and accuse me unjustly.
They repay me evil for good:
my soul is forlorn.

When they were sick I went into mourning,
afflicted with fasting.
My prayer was ever on my lips,
as for a brother, a friend.
I went as though mourning a mother,
bowed down with grief.

Now that I am in trouble they gather,
they gather and mock me.
They take me by surprise and strike me
and tear me to pieces.
They provoke me with mockery on mockery
and gnash their teeth.

O Lord, how long will you look on?
Come to my rescue!
Save my life from these raging beasts,
my soul from these lions.
I will thank you in the great assembly,
amid the throng I will praise you.

Do not let my lying foes
rejoice over me.
Do not let those who hate me unjustly
wink eyes at each other.

O Lord, you have seen, do not be silent,
do not stand afar off! Awake, stir to my defense,
to my cause, O God!

Let there be joy for those who love my cause.
Let them say without end:
"Great is the Lord who delights
in the peace of his servant."

> Then my tongue shall speak of your justice,
> all day long of your praise.

Here is a reading in the liturgy for the feast of St. John Vianney from one of his talks:

"My little children, reflect on these words: the Christian's treasure is not on earth but in heaven. Our thought, then, ought to be directed to where our treasure is. This is the glorious duty of man: to pray and to love. If you pray and love, that is where a man's happiness lies.

"Prayer is nothing else but union with God. When one has a heart that is pure and united with God, he is given a kind of serenity and sweetness that makes him ecstatic, a light that surrounds him with marvelous brightness. In this intimate union, God and the soul are fused together like two bits of wax that no one can ever pull apart. This union of God with a tiny creature is a lovely thing. It is a happiness beyond understanding.

"We had become unworthy to pray, but God in his goodness allowed us to speak with him. Our prayer is incense that gives him the greatest pleasure.

"My little children, your hearts are small, but prayer stretches them and makes them capable of loving God. Through prayer we receive a foretaste of heaven and something of paradise comes down upon us. Prayer never leaves us without sweetness. It is honey that flows into the soul and makes all things sweet. When we pray properly, sorrows disappear like snow before the sun."

The sung response prayer to this reading is:

"Our troubles pass quickly,
and their burden seems light
when we compare them to the weight of eternal glory
which far exceeds the burden of our suffering.

"No eye has seen, no ear heard,
nor has the heart of man conceived,
the marvels God has prepared for those who love him."

Epilogue

My trial began the Monday after Thanksgiving, 1989, and ended five days later. I was found innocent of the photo felony, guilty of the misdemeanors. I was sentenced and fined, and my bond was continued as the case was appealed in 1990. When the judge continued the bond I remained free on appeal after the date of Jan. 2, 1990. Life went on.

I continued to recite the prayers of the Liturgy of the Hours each day, attend Mass in the morning at St. Jude's church and sometimes late in the day at St. Marys. I continued to talk with Bishop Cosgrove weekly and enjoy my family and walk with my wife when the Ohio winter allows.

Work days were at Betterway. We had three homes for adults, one for men, one women, and a family home.

Another home opened for men or women with AIDS or the HIV positive virus.

The youth homes all changed. Boys and girls went on to other programs, including some group homes. Our foster homes were turned over to another agency and the youths in them remained there.

The Deli restaurant was phased out of Betterway's programs as the need for a presence in the downtown area was gone; the Search Shop expanded and the trolley, ropes course, and farm continue.

Not surprisingly, some of the adults in all the homes were former boys and girls in the youth homes. Some were back in the home where they were five, ten, even 20 years ago.

Perhaps our contribution was to reach into the lives of the four thousand boys and girls who lived here as teens at Betterway and offer some a place in our family as adults. I believe that truly effective social work in the lives of people like we had at Betterway must create a community that can last a lifetime.

Those 4,000 who were here are marrying, doubling their number, and having children, increasing the numbers more. We will continue to try to help those who need it.

At this time there are some sad parts in this story. I was a friend and counselor to the seven boys who testified against me in the trial. They had told me the secrets of their lives. I had listened to them for many hours, gotten them out of numerous troubles. One young man's father had been at Betterway and was later killed. I found the only photo of him the boy had ever seen and told him stories about his father.

Another boy was being tried for the rape of his young sister and I helped solve the case and prove he did not do it. He faced a long stay in an institution. Another boy was with us three separate times and I helped him accept his mother's alcoholism as something that would not go away. I helped another face the fact that his family would never take him back, but we took him back after he ran away, stealing our van to do so. He begged to come back.

Some are too embarrassed to see me now. Their access to me as a friend was temporarily destroyed.

This has been sad for them. It is also sad for the adults who testified against me. We had been friends. They kept in touch. They had happy memories of life with Betterway. They always asked about kids who had been here and were known to them.

A sad part for me has been the loss of my reputation in the eyes of the hundreds of people I worked with for 35 years in social agencies, and in my own community and other places. People are embarrassed to talk to me. They do not want to be seen with me.

All of this was brought on by people I have yet to really meet, people I never knew. Then there is the fact of the ending of the programs for youth at Betterway; the selling of the vans and other equipment, the closing of the Deli. The ending of so many pieces that took so long to build up.
And why did it end?

Because some people were tired of Betterway and tired of the kids who were part of Betterway. They wanted us out of

Elyria. Plus the excitement, plus the inner motives in each person involved. I will address all this in a book soon.

On the other hand, the enormity of these sadnesses and angers makes the challenge of surviving all the greater. It makes the effort to forgive all the more intense. And in these kinds of life struggles, we grow stronger and we move on to new heights because of it all.

During the 5 trial days I was often preoccupied by my worries about the people in our new AIDS program. It had only been open two months and we were still learning how to help these people who were so sick at times.

I sat in my chair, the jury on one side, my attorney before me, the prosecutor and detective across the table, friends, cameras, TV, people on the witness stand saying good things and bad things about me, the judge watching. All this drama and I was worrying about a person with AIDS who had taken off from us and needed a lot of hospital care. It seemed like this was all a waste of time in comparison with helping someone who was so sick.

At other times I thought of Christ on trial and how privileged I was to have this same experience. It filled me with a sense of joy, even when I heard the words "guilty" over and over. However my trial was so much more civilized than Christ's trial. I had it easier.

It seems that good came to me and to Betterway from all this. A blessing in disguise. And I feel sure that the future will prove this to be even more true than any of us realize now.

The Akathistos Hymn

The Akathistos Hymn is one of the most beautiful prayers honoring the Virgin Mary in all Christianity. Yet it is little known outside the Eastern Catholic and Orthodox churches.

The hymn was written in 626 A.D., over 1,300 years ago. It celebrates the occasion when the city of Constantinople was being attacked by the barbarian Persian navy and the people prayed to Mary to save them, marching in procession around their great city, carrying icons of Christ and His Mother and singing psalms.

A strong wind came up and blew the enemy ships off course. This historic hymn was composed in thanksgiving.

It is sung with psalms in the liturgy on Saturdays in Lent in Eastern Rite Christian churches. It has been used in private devotions by millions for centuries. It has been translated from the Greek original into many languages.

People who read the Akathistos Hymn seem to find new meaning in a phrase or sentence each time they use it in prayer. This modern translation should enrich many lives.

This translation by Tom Peters was the first book to be published by Betterpub Press, the Betterway Publishing Press.

◑ betterpubpress ◑
606 Middle Ave., Elyria, Ohio 44035
216-323-2431

$4.95

ISBN 1-879516-01-2